Finance for the Perplexed Executive

Ray Proctor is Deputy Director of the National Coal Board's South Wales Area. He joined the NCB in the late 1960s as a graduate trainee and has worked in a variety of finance posts in the Yorkshire and East Midlands coalfields and at the NCB's national headquarters. His interest in management development stems from a period as Director of Studies at the NCB's Staff College in the early 1980s. He is an Associate Member of the Institute of Cost and Management Accountants and Honorary Treasurer of the Association of Teachers of Management.

Other books for The Successful Manager

Managing Your Own Career, Dave Francis
Manage Your Time, Sally Garratt
Managing Yourself, Mike Pedler and Tom Boydell
The Roots of Excellence, Ronnie Lessem

Ray Proctor

Finance for the Perplexed Executive

Fontana/Collins

First published in 1986 by Fontana Paperbacks
and simultaneously in hardback by William Collins
8 Grafton Street, London W1X 3LA

Hardback ISBN:0 00217771 4
Paperback ISBN:0 00637048 9

Set in Linotron Times
Made and printed in Great Britain by
William Collins Sons & Co. Ltd, Glasgow

To Pauline

Contents

Introduction

Gwyn Thomas, a son of the Rhondda, claimed for the Welsh a special form of genius. They could take a doleful hymn like 'From Greenland's Icy Wastes' and make it sound like a Latin American rumba. A similar skill is required in writing a 'popular' book on such an apparently baleful theme as Managerial Finance. To most managers this is a subject which could bore a glass eye to sleep. Just as you don't join a monastery to meet girls, you hardly pick up a book on Managerial Finance and expect to be entertained. For when managers come to compile the definitive *Atlas of Business Studies*, the tropical zones will be occupied by the Behavioural Sciences and the Human Side of Enterprise – hot, steamy themes developed with damp passion to the rhythm of jungle drums. In the temperate zones are located the cooler, more restrained subjects – Marketing, Business Policy, Quantitative Techniques. Here the sounds are less piercing, the sights less exotic, the smells less pungent. This is a decent place in which to live and bring up children. And finally, at the polar extremities, stuck in the tundra, deep in permafrost, we find Managerial Finance. Managers approach these glacial regions of knowledge with all the enthusiasm of a man about to handle a dead snake. At best they fear boredom, at worst frostbite, chilblains and hypothermia.

But this is not an academic book on finance. It is not a textbook, groaning with examples, questions and model answers at the back. Nor is it a 'teach yourself' manual with blank spaces to be filled in and checked against the correct answers. The intention is not to convert non-financial managers into accountants. After all, Ireland remains the most pious of nations although, in two thousand years, there has not been a single Irish Pope. Nor is it the *Thirty-Microsecond Accountant*, a script for bluffing your way through your next accountability meeting, a Christmas tree decked out with buzz-words, flavours of the month and techniques with the lifespan of your average mayfly. In terms of getting your whiskers ahead in the rat race, this book will not even bring you to the starting line. What follows is verbal Warfarin to all rodent activity.

The objective of this book is to widen the non-financial manager's perspective of managerial finance and to provide a better understanding of the financial phenomena which have an impact on his or her job. We are concerned not with the fine detail but with the broad sweep. Our concern, as they say on Barnsley market-place, is with the *gestalt*. I freely confess that, in seeking to clarify and to reduce tedium, I have taken a measure of poetic licence in the more prosaic aspects of the subject. Graham Greene distinguishes, in his writings, between 'novels' and 'entertainments'. In the Great Academic Library of Financial Knowledge this book will be indexed as an 'entertainment' and may well be banished to the shelves marked 'fiction'. But, in the words of John Locke, 'in an age that produces such masters as the great Huygenius and the incomparable Mr Newton . . . it is ambition enough to be employed as an underlabourer in clearing the ground a little and removing some of the rubbish that lies in the way to knowledge'.

And this is where the punters, the Perplexed Executives, come wandering on to the set. They have been trained as single-function specialists – engineers, computer scientists, lawyers, personnel managers. They are 'in' sales, training, advertising, provisioning, public relations, line management, industrial relations, research and development. As they develop in these specialisms they identify linkages with, and acquire knowledge of, other specialisms, which impinge on their own. In this process of development they may even penetrate to the sunlit uplands of general management. But in this process of intellectual expansion, one specialism tends to remain unpenetrated, the financial specialism. To many executives this specialism conforms to Churchill's description of Soviet Russia, 'a mystery wrapped in a riddle and enveloped by an enigma'. And this is perplexing because the financial dimension seems to have an impact upon all the specialisms within the firm. More pertinently, the executive is expected to understand and to interpret financial information as part of the job. But relatively simple concepts, like the difference between cash flow and profit, investment appraisal techniques and the impact of inflation on financial results, remain obscure. The executive is faced with a dilemma. Does he admit to ignorance and risk being reviled? Or does he pretend to knowledge and risk exposure? The executive is thoroughly perplexed. Like most people in the modern world, he is too honest to tell a lie but too smart to tell the truth . . . This book offers a route out of perplexity. Its simple aim is to enable the executive to feel comfortable with the major financial concepts.

This book is not a crusade to save the world for finance and accountancy. It is not my intention to lie down and bleed for the latter profession. It is self-evident that the financial dimension is important in the operations of any firm. In the lean years of the 1980s most firms are faced with infinite demands on finite resources. Reconciliation is achieved through prioritization and allocation and these processes are often based on financial criteria. If the executive wishes both to understand and to influence the process, then, as Wittgenstein suggests, he must 'first learn the language'.

The firm, then, is influenced by finance's magnetic field. But finance is not the only influence nor, in many cases, is it the most important influence. The limitations of financial information and, indeed, of rationality in general need constantly to be stressed. Profit is an effect not a cause. Financial information will analyze price and cost in great detail but has difficulty with concepts like value. The balance sheet quantifies working capital and fixed assets in considerable detail but is totally silent on the firm's most valuable assets: the skills, knowledge and experience of those who work in it.

The book is designed as a downmarket Baedeker, a guide to the strange land of finance. We start with a lightning tour of the financial territory and note that it is a civilization based on the concept of cash. We learn the language of the territory and examine the concepts and conventions which infuse the meaning of this language. We observe the main topographical features of the territory, the balance sheet, Profit and Loss Account and cash flow statement. We ponder how best this territory might be managed in terms of systems and units of administration. We then explore the territory's four major regions, the Profit and Loss Account, working capital, capital structure and fixed assets. We look at capital investment appraisal in theory and in practice and concur that hindsight is the only perfect science. We then examine techniques which enable the territory, in whole and in part, to be monitored and controlled. Finally, we observe the inhabitants of this strange land. We see them responding to change in both the financial and social environment. We consider the results, inflation accounting and social accounting. We end with some observations on how the non-financial executive can come to terms with his financial confrères, how the lion can lie down with the lamb. And if, at the end of the journey, the non-financial executive is none the wiser, at least he or she will be better informed.

1. The Territory of Finance

To a business, cash is like a pair of lungs: the business needs it if it wants to go on breathing. The history of industry and commerce is pitted with examples of firms which simply stopped breathing because the cash ran out – Rolls Royce, BLMC, EMI, Dunlop. And if the black box could be recovered from the ruins of many other corporate disasters, the pilot's last words would be unmistakeable: 'Bills to pay, no cash to pay 'em. Bank unsympathetic.' Nation states, like businesses, also need lungs and, in recent times, the indebtedness of Latin American and Eastern European countries has put the lifesupport machines of international credit on overtime. As recently as 1976, the United Kingdom itself was subjected to the indignity of an economic enema before receiving its whiffs of oxygen from the International Monetary Fund. But it was not always thus . . .

For nearly three centuries the imperial route to India lay round the Cape of Good Hope. An overland link between the Mediterranean and the Red Sea, by barge and carriage, had been established in the 1840s by the Peninsular and Oriental Steamship Company but the venture had met with scant success. From time to time, the construction of a canal was proposed but in London such proposals were dismissed, with a mixture of imperial hauteur and vested interest, as dubious engineering prospects. Quite simply, it could not be done!

So it came as a bit of a blow to the imperial selfesteem when, in 1869, the Suez Canal opened for business. Quite apart from *amour propre*, the problem for the British was that the Canal's constructor, De Lesseps, was a Frenchman, the Suez Canal Company was based in Paris and the opening ceremony was performed not by the Empress Victoria but by the Empress Eugénie. The British reacted like Swiss watchmakers confronted with their first

13

Japanese digital watch or English brewers at their initial tasting of continental lager. This Canal was an interesting, even ingenious little concept. But it would never catch on!

By 1875, the facts no longer fitted the theory. The Canal had been a great success. Benjamin Disraeli and his Cabinet were in something of a sweat. In its short life, the Canal had become the spinal cord of the Empire but the fingers which fondled the spine were Gallic, not Anglo-Saxon. But what to do? A gunboat, an infiltration of missionaries, an exhibition of Victorian artefacts in the shadow of the Sphinx? No. A solution was required which would be politically and managerially effective. As Machiavelli astutely observed, in *The Prince*: 'Those who wish to win favour with a Prince customarily offer him those things which . . . they see him most delight in.'

The Prince in question was the Khedive, ruler of Egypt in the deeply fissured Ottoman Empire. In what did the Khedive most delight? Greenbacks. His 40 per cent holding in the Compagnie Universelle du Canal Maritime was up for grabs. All that was required was £130 million, pronto and in readies. Now in the days of balanced budgets and sound finance, governments were simply not holding that sort of folding. Disraeli merely sent his Private Secretary round to have a word with his chum, Baron Edmund de Rothschild. Somewhat overawed, the emissary came to the point:

ROTHSCHILD: 'When?'
PRIVATE SECRETARY: 'Tomorrow.'
ROTHSCHILD *(pausing to eat a Muscatel grape and spit out the skin)*: 'What is your security?'
PRIVATE SECRETARY: 'The British Government.'
ROTHSCHILD: 'You shall have it'.
(Exit Private Secretary squelching grape skins.)

But, unfortunately, few businessmen these days have a friendly Baron Edmund de Rothschild in the office cupboard. Recession, and its concomitant shock, trauma and shrinkage, has made the old lungs work harder and white knights are an endangered species. And in the subconscious of the most recession-proof entrepreneur lurks the image of those Friday mornings long ago when the young secretary would be sent to the bank to charm money out of an empty account. In her absence, as the employees hovered outside the office muttering about wages, the embryonic entrepreneur would sink to his knees and pray to the Almighty that she be not allowed to return empty-handed.

Cash is the proper preoccupation of business and cash, in all its manifestations, forms the territory of finance. The territory has its own specialized language, the language of finance, and its topography is characterized by a series of dominating features – the balance sheet, the Profit and Loss Account (income statement), the Sources and Uses of Funds Statement. These features, in turn, have their own detailed geology – assets and liabilities, revenues and expenses, inflows and outflows. Like all civilized lands, the territory needs a modicum of management. Systems and techniques have been duly devised for this purpose. The fabric of the territory needs to be maintained, renewed and extended: choices must be made amongst alternatives. Again, the territory has forged the appropriate tools. And the territory is not immune to the turbulence of modern times. It has developed mechanisms for survival. But, at the sap-centre of all these ramifications, is one simple commodity, cash. An appreciation of the financial function in any firm must start with an understanding of the firm as a *dynamic cash model*.

The easiest route to such an understanding lies through fantasy, the fantasy of the menopausal manager who is still interested in the ladies of the typing-pool but can't remember why. As he luxuriates in the comfortable womb of the large corporation, musing on annual increments and index-linked pensions, he is struck by a realization that time is passing him by. Enough of golden parachutes and mink-lined landing pads! Break out of the foetal position! Clamber out of the cellar of your mind and dare to be great! 'Tis time to go it alone and start your own business.

In turning fantasy into reality, you learn your first lesson. *You are not Benjamin Disraeli!* You can call upon neither the friendship of Eddie de Rothschild nor the security of HMG. Your needs at this seminal stage are neatly encapsulated in a simple equation:

PMA+OPM = SUCCESS

PMA? 'Positive Mental Attitude'. Fantasy *can* be turned into reality. Scaling the North Face of the Eiger is no more than a gentle stroll in the hills. It *is* possible to produce a baby in one month by simultaneously impregnating nine women. OPM? 'Other People's Money'. We are back to the bedrock of cash. But how is the M. to be prised from OP's reluctant grasp?

In general terms, OPM comes in three forms – share capital, loan capital and grants. The two former, share capital and loan capital, have not changed much since Disraeli's day. Indeed, the progenitor of the Limited Liability or Joint Stock Company, the Companies Act of 1862, reached the statute books when Disraeli's political star was still rising. The third form of OPM, grant aid from central and local government, is a more recent phenomenon, a function of the Keynesian revolution and the managed economy. Queen Victoria would not have approved but Disraeli, the 'new conservative', would have understood.

Share capital is the permanent capital of the firm and generally comes in the shape of ordinary shares ('equity capital'). The cash brought into the firm reflects the issue price of the shares, not the nominal value or the price quoted on the Stock Exchange, Unlisted Securities Market or private placement. Hence, in February 1982, the Radiochemical Centre was 'privatized' as Amersham International. Fifty million shares with a nominal value of 25p per share were offered to the public at an issue price of 142p per share. Within days, the shares were quoted on the London Stock Exchange at 190p per share. In terms of cash brought into the firm, the only relevant figure is the issue price. Capital appreciation, though not without its benefits, pays no bills for the company at this stage. Shareholders are not 'creditors' (people to whom the firm owes money) but 'owners' of the firm. It is to these owners that the management of the firm 'renders account' through the medium of the Annual Report and Accounts. As owners, the shareholders participate in the benefits of success through dividend (the cost of share capital to the firm) and capital appreciation of their ordinary shares. But, with doleful symmetry, they must also bear the prime risk of failure. If the firm founders, they will be left with the residue of the assets (or not) after the creditors have been satisfied (or not). The residue is often no more than a puff of rancid air.

Loans represent the semi-permanent capital of the business. They lack permanence in the capital structure because at some future date they will fall due for repayment in part or in whole. The interest rate, fixed or floating, represents the cost of borrowing. The loan will usually entail the provision of security fixed on a specific asset (your house, the company's premises) or as a general floating charge on the company's assets. In the business start-up situation, there is some evidence that the provision of security rather than the interest rate payable is the major impediment to entrepreneurial endeavour. The providers of loans are not owners but creditors of the firm. Loans themselves represent a 'liability' (a legal obligation to pay a fixed amount at a specified time in return for a current benefit).

With all this, the good Baron Edmund de Rothschild would have been familiar. But he would have gagged on his grape, flabber well and truly gasted, at the cornucopia of financial assistance now available from central and local government. Islwyn Borough Council in the County of Gwent, South Wales, recently listed the following financial incentives for companies starting or re-locating in the borough:

Regional Development Grants: at 22% or 15% of capital expenditure on buildings and machinery.

Selective Financial Assistance: discretionary grants on capital expenditure to create new jobs and safeguard existing jobs.

Office and Service Industry Grants: job-related grants available within assisted areas and help for key-workers to move.

Contracts Preference Scheme: favouring firms based in Special and Development Areas.

European Grants and Loans: low interest loans from the European Investment Bank and the European Coal and

Steel Community and grants from the European Social Fund.

Employment Transfer Scheme: grants for assisting employees to travel to seek work.

Export Grants: towards marketing research and development costs of export markets.

Tax Allowances: on industrial buildings and machinery.

Local Authority Grants and Mortgages: relating to industrial sites and buildings.

Now all this may seem as Byzantine as British Rail's fare-structure but it reflects a Keynesian commitment to full employment and regional policy. In 1984, the rate of adult male unemployment in Islwyn was in excess of 20 per cent. But grants represent a transitory rather than a permanent or semi-permanent form of capital. They are, by and large, one-off infusions of cash.

So whether in the form of share capital, loans or grants, the OPM flows into our fledgling firm. It's now time to call the PMA into play and test the fledgling's wings.

The first call on the cash will probably be for investment in 'fixed assets' (resources with a relatively long economic life, acquired not for resale or conversion directly into a product but for use in producing other goods and services). Fixed assets usually comprise such items as land, buildings, plant and machinery, fittings and fixtures, vehicles, etc. Investment in such items is categorized as 'capital expenditure'.

Secondly, cash is required for the acquisition of 'current assets' (assets expected to be converted into cash or consumed within twelve months or the normal operating cycle). At the pre-start stage, a manufacturing concern would require stocks of raw materials, a retail outlet would need a stock-in-trade. Current assets when consumed in the business (raw materials) or converted directly into cash (stock-in-trade) represent 'revenue expenditure'.

In a manufacturing concern, a body press is obviously a fixed asset and its acquisition represented capital expenditure. But the sheet steel held in stock for processing through the machine is a current asset and, when processed, represents revenue expenditure. The display unit in a retail outlet is a fixed asset (capital): the goods it displays are current assets (revenue). More metaphysically, it has been suggested that the brain is a fixed asset while the ideas which circulate therein are current assets.

Thirdly, cash is required to meet operational expenses which do not involve the acquisition of either fixed or current assets. Such time-related items as rent, rates and insurance premia will need to be settled in advance. Wages and salaries may become payable before production gets underway. Again, these items are further examples of revenue expenditure.

Fourthly, a modicum of cash needs to be retained in easily accessible form to enable the firm to hang loose. Cash is needed as a hedge against the unexpected, 'the rainy day syndrome', and to provide the flexibility to make a positive response to windfall situations – the sudden availability of cheap supplies, plant at discount prices.

The cash brought into the firm in the form of share capital, loans or grants is gradually turned into assets, fixed and current, and disbursed as operational expenses.

And now the fledgling is ready to make its own way in the world. The firm duly starts to make its product or provide its service. In the manufacturing concern, raw materials are drawn from stock and applied to the fixed assets and a range of operational expenses incurred. From the end of the track, finished products begin to flow. These products can either be stocked or sold ex-works to the customer. If stocked, the finished products form a species of current asset, 'finished goods'. Such stocks contain inputs of direct labour and materials on which expenditure has been incurred. As such, the stocks represent cash tied up in the firm. But even if the finished products in their entirety are sold straight off the production line, a simultaneous inflow of cash is not necessarily generated. Similarly, outflows of cash are not necessarily contemporaneous with the acquisition of assets or the incurring of operating expenses. We are discovering the miracle of credit.

On the input side, the typical firm does not settle with its suppliers of resources immediately and in cash. It takes a period of credit from the suppliers of fixed assets and raw materials. It also usually receives such credit from its employees. Typically, wages and salaries are paid in arrears. If your salary is paid monthly on the last day of the month, as the month progresses you are a creditor ('a person to whom the firm owes money') of the firm for an ever increasing amount. Creditors, like shareholders and the providers of loans, are financing the business: they are providing the firm with the use of their cash for the due period of credit. Theoretically, through the miracle of credit, it is possible for our firm to start up and have its product in the market before parting with any of the cash raised in the form of permanent and semi-permanent capital.

But, in the territory of finance, for every credit there is a debit. On the outputs side, the firm experiences the obverse of the process. Having received credit on its inputs, the firm is faced with extending credit to its customers on its outputs. And it is not simply the dictates of symmetry and natural justice which encourage the extension of such credit. Terms of payment, like price, quality and availability, form part of the marketing appeal of the product. But the provision of credit to customers ties up cash in 'debtors' ('people who owe us money'). Here the firm is providing the customer with the use of its cash. Debtors, like stocks, represent another species of current asset. The debts will be duly converted into cash but only then will the cash actually flow back into the firm. Sales do not necessarily produce an immediate infusion of cash.

So permanent and semi-permanent capital in the form of shares and loans, together with a one-off injection of grants, has provided the firm with its initial grubstake. Fixed and current assets have been acquired and operational expenses incurred. To the extent that these asset acquisitions and operational expenses have not been settled in cash, a body of creditors has been created. Until such settlement is made, the creditors are providing the firm with finance and calls upon the grubstake are minimized. Only when settlement takes place does cash physically flow out of the firm. Conversely, cash flows into the firm only when the period of credit provided by the firm expires and the debtors settle their bills.

Current Assets (stock, cash and debtors) minus Creditors is usually known as the 'working capital' of the firm. Working capital is sometimes referred to as the 'net current assets' of the firm: the terms are synonymous. Neither expression contains the flavour of the term used by the Victorians. Baron Edmund de Rothschild would have known working capital as 'circulating capital', a term which neatly distinguishes it from 'fixed' assets and captures the dynamism of the process.

It is essential that this dynamism is appreciated. We have seen that the flow of cash out of the firm via creditors is not necessarily synchronized or symmetrical with the flow of cash back into the firm via debtors. The concept of cash velocity is important. The slower the cash leaves the business to settle amounts owed to creditors, and the quicker the cash moves back into the business from the customer, the less the demand on the grubstake to support working capital. But, as usual in this imperfect world, the real falls well short of the ideal. Our fledgling firm, with no track record and a credit rating of zero triple minus, will receive little credit from its suppliers. Cash on delivery will be the order of the day. Conversely, as a newcomer to the marketplace, the customer may need to be lubricated with long lines of credit. The way of progress is uphill and against the wind. The result can be considerable sums of cash tied up in working capital just when the firm needs to hang loose.

Even when the fledgling grows to maturity, the ideal can prove just as illusory. By and large, creditors are a function of production and debtors a function of sales. If production and sales become uncoupled by a sudden fall in market demand and production cannot be quickly scaled down, stocks will rise and working capital requirements increase. Again, the bio-rhythms of normal trading can make heavy demands on working capital. Seasonal peaking of demand can entail many months producing solely for stock with a build-up of working capital before the tidal wave of cash comes crashing back into the firm after the period of peak demand. If the tide stays obstinately out, you know how

Clive Sinclair felt in the early months of 1985. Products with long lead-times can produce similar contours: ship-building, civil engineering and capital goods generally cause a swelling of the working capital in the gestation period.

But, in some circumstances, the pattern of cash inflows and outflows can be made to work to the firm's advantage. The retail sector is a good example. The scale of the order placed with the supplier demands extended credit terms. An efficient distribution, stock-holding and merchandizing system expedites the goods through the check-out point before the period of credit has expired. And if the sale is for cash or near-cash, the cash actually flows into the firm well before it needs to be re-directed to the supplier. A glance at the published accounts of many retailers reveals the phenomenon of 'negative working capital'. The finance supplied by creditors exceeds the amount of cash tied up in current assets. The supplier is not only financing the working capital of the firm, he is also helping to fund its fixed assets. And he is doing all this free and gratis.

Imbalances, then, between cash inflows and cash outflows will occur in the normal course of trading operations. Such imbalances, in a healthy firm, are of an essentially short-term nature. To offset a temporary shortfall, short-term finance will be brought into the firm via an overdraft facility, a short-term loan or such devices as factoring. When the firm finds itself with a temporary cash suplus, cash, like any other asset, needs to earn its keep. Usually the money will be invested, short-term, outside the firm. The investment will be made in assets with high 'liquidity' ('able to be turned into cash very quickly') so that the cash can be summoned back into the firm at the first sign that feast is turning into famine.

And if our firm is successful, revenues will exceed expenses and a profit will be struck. Some of this profit will be distributed via creditors to shareholders in the form of dividend and to the Inland Revenue in the form of tax. The balance will be retained within the firm. 'Retained profit' provides an additional source of funds for the firm, but, unlike loans and shares, it is internally, not externally, generated. Where such internally generated funds are inadequate to maintain or expand fixed assets and working capital, additional external funds must be brought into the firm and the wheel of fortune starts another cycle.

The movements of cash round this cycle provide the territory of finance with its ground-plan (Figure 1). The initial grubstake is brought into the firm from the issue of shares (1) and the raising of loans (2). Fixed and current assets are acquired and operational expenses incurred. Insofar as credit transactions are involved, cash flows out of the firm via creditors (3). But the assets and the operational expenditure generate a product or service which is sold (4). To the extent that the sales are for credit, not cash, debtors are created (5). When the debtor pays up, cash flows back into the firm (6). Temporary cash shortfalls are met by short-term loans/overdrafts (7), surpluses by short-term investments outside

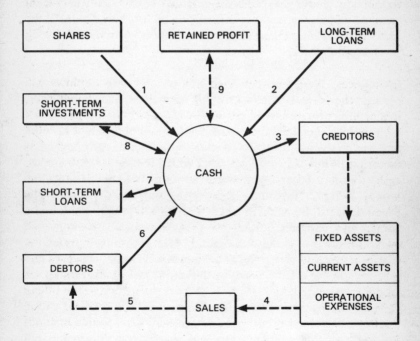

Figure 1: *The firm as a dynamic cash model*

the firm (8). If revenues exceed expenses, profits are made and a proportion is retained within the firm as an internally generated source of funds (9).

The dynamic cash model of the firm provides the territory of finance with its ground plan. But it is essential to appreciate the dynamism contained within the static delineations of the plan. At any one time, cash is moving through the system in myriad different forms. And, within the dynamism, there is a cyclical process. Cash comes swimming into the system, struggles through the production process, is stranded in the Sargasso Sea of debtors but finally, the debt duly settled, like a salmon battling back to its spawning grounds, reappears in the familiar waters of the firm to start the process all over again.

2. The Language of the Financial Territory

'And I lifted up my eyes and, behold, a man with a measuring line in his hand.'

Zechariah ii, 1

The sheer dynamism of the cash model of the firm, with cash metamorphosed through a variety of identities, makes the model an inappropriate vehicle for the expression, monitoring and control of the firm's financial position and performance. If the dynamism is not recognized, we find ourselves trying to force moving phenomena into a static framework, a process similar to fitting a jumper on to an octopus or nailing a globule of mercury to the floor. In this situation, the accountant's role is similar to that of the surveyor: both are concerned with measurement, the one with the financial world, the other with the physical world. For both, objects, whether physical or financial, are easier to measure when at repose rather than when in motion. So, for purposes of analysis, monitoring and control, the dynamic model has to be stopped and static readings taken. These readings provide a snapshot of the firm in financial terms at one point in time. The snapshot has value in itself as a record of one precise moment in the firm's life and, when compared with older photographs in the firm's family album, points up changes over time.

Static readings are required for three main purposes:

(i) to delineate the financial position of the firm at the time of the reading: financial position is delineated by measuring assets and liabilities (what it owns and what it owes). The balance sheet performs this function.

(ii) to determine the financial performance of the firm: financial performance is determined by measuring revenues and expenses which have arisen since the time of the previous snapshot. The Profit and Loss Account performs this function.

(iii) to detail the liquidity of the firm, its generation and absorption of cash: liquidity is detailed by measuring cash outgoings and incomings since the time of the previous snapshot. The Sources and Uses of Funds Statement serves this need. The balance sheet, Profit and Loss Account and Sources and Uses of Funds Statement are the three major instruments of financial measurement.

Before we examine these instruments, it is necessary to ponder further on the problems posed by freezing the dynamic model and interpreting the resultant snapshot. For, in stopping the dynamic model, there is not the cause and effect relationship of throwing a switch and transforming a throbbing piece of machinery into instant stillness and silence. Some parts of the model refuse to be stilled, others adopt inappropriate or unphotogenic poses. Some parts are off the site when the photographer calls, others seem to have strayed on to the wrong set. Some hard, lumpy objects in the firm refuse to be defined either as stocks of raw material or as stocks of finished product but lie around in semi-finished form – cars without engines, books without covers, Action Men without flak jackets. How is their value to be measured? Machines figure in the photograph. They obviously have value but how is this value to be defined? Initial cost? Re-saleable value? Replacement cost? Services may have been consumed and the benefits appear for us all to see. But no bill has been received at the time of the photo-call. Do we need to touch up the print for such omissions? Conversely, we may have incurred substantial up-front costs to secure an order which has not yet materialized. Are we to include both the cost and the benefit? Include the former but not the latter? Banish both from the shot? And what about the people in the picture? Do we try to put a financial value on the knowledge, skills and experience of the people in the firm? Or do we borrow the KGB's airbrush and erase them from the scene?

To resolve these and other issues, the territory of finance has developed its own specialized language. For its syntax the language relies upon a series of esoteric concepts and conventions. The three major instruments of financial measurement – balance sheet, Profit and Loss Account, Sources and Uses of Funds Statement – are only fully comprehensible in terms of this specialized language and its syntax. We must enter the language laboratory.

The syntax contains seven major concepts and three major conventions. These are outlined below. First the concepts, then the conventions . . .

1. Dual aspect

The concept of the dual aspect holds that 'at all times the assets of the firm must equal its liabilities or "equities" (claims against assets by owners or creditors).' The concept gives rise to the 'double-entry' system of book-keeping. Double-entry systems first emerged in Florence in the late thirteenth century. The concept (*partita doppia*) was duly codified by the Franciscan friar Luca Pacioli in his book *De Arithmetica* published in 1496. Some scholars have attributed epoch-making properties to the concept and have compared its influence on the development of rationalism with the systems of Galileo and Newton. The German historian Spengler considered *partita doppia* to be seminal in the emergence of capitalism. 'It is simply impossible to imagine capitalism without double-entry book-keeping: they are like form and content'. Now, even allowing for a spot of academic hyperbole, all this seems a trifle overblown. Can we really class double-entry book-keeping alongside revisionism and Yankee imperialism as the true enemies of the working class? Does Luca Pacioli rank with Adolph Hitler and Leon Trotsky in the demon-ology of Marxism-Leninism? Surely not. The concept is important in the syntax of the language of finance. But to ascribe more global properties to it is to confuse the scaffolding with the building.

Double-entry book-keeping confuses and thoroughly bores most non-financial managers but the principle of the dual aspect is relatively straightforward. It works as follows:

(a) We borrow £10k from the Midland Bank: we have thereby created a liability on the firm to the bank in the sum of £10k.

However, the same transaction has simultaneously provided us with an asset, namely, £10k lining the office safe or deposited in the firm's bank account. At one and the same time we have both an asset and a liability and the one is equal to the other. Hence, our books of account would show:

	Liabilities		Assets
	£k		£k
Loan	10	Bank Account	10
		(or cash)	

(b)   We use the £10k, one day later, to buy goods valued at £10k. We place the goods in stock with a view to resale. We have replaced one asset (bank account or cash) with another asset (stocks) of an equivalent value. The liability to the Midland Bank remains unaffected. The dual aspect is maintained and the position is as follows:

	Liabilities		Assets
	£k		£k
Loan	10	Stocks	10

(c)   We now make our sale. We sell the goods from stock at a price of £15k. Payment is immediate and in cash. The cash is simply deposited in the firm's safe. The liability to the Midland Bank remains but we appear, at first sight, to have lost contact with the dual aspect:

	Liabilities		Assets
	£k		£k
Loan	10	Cash	15

Contact is re-established if we analyze the £15k which we realized on sale. £10k represents the cost of the goods, the balance (£5k) being profit. The profit is, in fact, an 'equity'. It represents a claim, in the sum of £5k, which the owners of the firm, the shareholders, properly have on the assets of the firm. The true position on completion of the sale is. . .

	Liabilities		Assets
	£k		£k
Loan	10	Cash	15
Reserve	5		
(profit)			
	15		15

The integrity of the dual aspect is maintained. For every credit there is a debit.

2. Money measurement

'Accounting records show only facts which can be expressed in monetary terms.' Now here we are into epoch-making material. For what this seemingly innocent concept implies is that a financial value should not be put upon the skills, knowledge and experience of the firm's human resources. This implication causes much *angst* among those concerned with the human side of the organization. The scene is set for a modern, managerial morality play:

ENLIGHTENED MANAGER: 'The most valuable asset which this firm can deploy is the human resource, the rich and varied talent, experience and dedication of all those who work for the firm, from shop floor to boardroom. It is this asset, not the materials and machines, the nuts and bolts, the amps and volts, which crucially determines our current performance and future prospects. Men are the masters of machines, not vice versa. Yet it is precisely this, the most important asset, which is missing from the accountant's view of the world. You accountants portray a 'neutron bomb' view of the world, the people have been obliterated but the land and buildings, plant and machinery remain intact and in excellent repair. On behalf of the caring managerial professions I invite the accountants to rejoin the human race.'

(*Applause from the Caring Professions*)

ACCOUNTANT (*selects from his intellectual quiver the shaft marked 'sweet reason' – begins to speak to faint hisses*): 'Colleague, our difference is one of semantics, not ideology. We accountants fully endorse your encomium on the human side of the organization. We too are caring, sensitive people. However, you must remember that the language of finance is an esoteric tongue and in this tongue the word "asset" is used in a specialized sense to mean "things which we own". Do you really wish to categorize the human resource in such terms of bondage? If you do, shall we classify the human resource as a "fixed asset"? The human resource can then take its place alongside plant and machinery, fixtures and fittings, land and buildings. Or would you prefer to classify ourselves and our colleagues in the firm as "current assets" (assets expected to be converted into cash or consumed in the business within twelve months or the normal operating cycle)? We can then rank ourselves with oils and greases, piles of coal and cans of beans.' (*Moves from defence to attack, from born-again liberal to stern pragmatist*). 'And if we are to revise and rewrite the language of finance to accommodate this special class of human asset, how is it to be valued? On an individual basis? Are we to treat employees as soccer players and assign to each a notional value derived from a hypothetical transfer fee? Are free transfers permissible? Can certain individuals' (*pointed stare at enlightened manager*) 'be assigned a negative value? If so, who is to tell them? Will appeals be allowed to a Human Resource Valuation Tribunal? Or should standard values be allocated to each specialism and function? £20k per accountant, £10k per engineer, £1k per personnel manager? The money measurement concept exists to avoid the exercise of subjective judgement in a language designed to be objective.'
(*Exit enlightened manager, lost for words.*)

What the enlightened manager did not know was that the National City Bank of New York came close to a valuation system for certain of its employees in the early 1930s. Each year, a proportion of the bank's profits were paid into a fund for disbursement to the principal officers of the firm. But who was to get what and who was to decide? Athenian democracy provided the answer. Each principal officer wrote on a ballot slip the amount he considered each of his fellow officers to be worth. Common decency precluded self-valuation. The ballot slips, unsigned, were dropped into a ballot box. The values assigned to each individual were aggregated and the aggregation divided by the number of ballot slips. The result determined individual shares of the loot.

3. Historical cost

The historical cost concept follows on from money measurement. It defines the 'money terms' under which the 'facts' are to be recorded. 'Assets are, in normal circumstances, entered on accounting records at the price paid to acquire them.' When an asset, fixed or current, is acquired by the firm, it is valued at what it cost the firm to acquire it. This cost, verifiable from invoices and other prime sources, is a matter of objective fact and is not conditioned by subjective value judgements. Now the enlightened manager may mutter about knowing the cost of everything and the value of nothing, but the historical cost concept does introduce 'hardness' into what could be a very 'soft' area.

Under the historical cost concept, when we buy a fixed asset like a machine, the amount which we have paid is duly recorded. An estimate is made of the useful economic life of the machine. The historical cost ('the value') is written down ('reduced') throughout that useful life. The annual amount by which the value is written down is the 'depreciation' charge on that machine.

Assume that the machine was acquired for £10k and that its useful economic life was assessed at five years. The annual depreciation charge ('straight line method') is calculated by dividing the historical cost by the useful life. This produces an annual depreciation charge of £2k. So, one year after acquisition, the machine will have a 'written-down value' (WDV) in the firm's accounting records of £8k. As we shall see in the next chapter, depreciation is retained within the firm and represents a source of internally generated funds. Hence, by the end of the machine's useful life, accumulated depreciation in the sum of £10k (the historical cost) will have been retained in the firm theoretically for the replacement of the defunct machine. The system is based on the recovery of the historical cost and implies a rough symmetry between historical cost and replacement price.

Until the early 1970s, it was (just) possible to argue that such a rough symmetry did indeed prevail. Thereafter, double digit inflation blew the argument right out of the water. With it went the sanctity of the historical cost concept. The problems of 'accounting for inflation' are considered in Chapter 10.

4. Business entity

'Accounts are kept for business entities and not for the persons associated with those entities.' The company is in law a different person altogether from the members of the company; it has its own legal and corporate personality. The concept is, in many ways, a throwback to Victorian times when the sole proprietorship was a common form of business organization. With the division of ownership from management, the concept no longer has great currency. However, in the era of 'enterprise' and growth through the development of small business, with the proliferation of small consultancies and the growth of 'knowledge' businesses, the concept could have renewed relevance. The groundrules were established in the case of *Salomon* v. *Salomon* (1897).

5. Going concern

'Accounting treatment assumes that a business will continue indefinitely and is not about to be sold.' Value is a relative concept. Where a firm is subject to a takeover bid, a number of quite different 'values' can be isolated. There is the value of the offer made for the firm. There is the value of the firm's issued shares prior to the takeover bid. And there is the value of the firm's assets as shown in its balance sheet. The three values are based on entirely different considerations. The value of the bid reflects the value of the firm to the bidder. The value of the issued shares reflects the market's views on income and capital appreciation possibilities. What concerns the accountant is the third value, the balance sheet valuation of the firm's assets. As we have seen, this valuation is made on the specialized accounting base of historical cost. This valuation takes no cognisance of the possibility that the firm might be about to be sold.

6. Realization concept

'Revenue is recognized in the accounting period in which it is realized, that is, in the accounting period during which goods are actually despatched or services rendered to the customer.' This concept becomes more comprehensible if examined in conjunction with the . . .

7. Accrual concept

'Profit or loss is measured as the difference between revenues and expenses rather than as the difference between cash receipts and cash disbursements.'

The realization and accrual concepts are of fundamental importance in the understanding of much financial information. In particular the concepts help to draw out the differences between the notion of 'profit' and the notion of 'cash'. The concepts also provide a further means of making static sense of the dynamic cash model of the firm. So what do the concepts mean?

Let's start on the sales side of the firm and focus on Accounting Period (AP) 1, four weeks in duration. In this accounting period sales will be made, goods will be despatched to customers and cash will flow into the firm. However, the cash which flows in is not necessarily attributable to the sales made and the goods despatched in AP 1. Assume that the firm is selling all its product on twenty-eight days' credit. If every customer plays the Boy Scout and settles on the due date, all the cash which flowed into the firm in AP 1 would be attributable not to sales made in AP 1 but to sales made in AP 12 of the previous financial year. By the same logic, sales made in AP 1 will not be translated into cash until AP 2. At the end of AP 1, the cash attributable to sales in that period will be represented in the firm's books as a current asset, debtors. The process is illustrated in Figure 2.

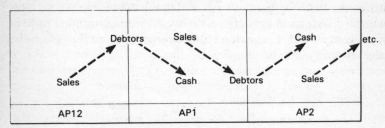

Figure 2: *The cash collection process*

We wish to measure the firm's financial performance in AP 1. To calculate profit or loss, we need to compare revenues in the period with expenses. The realization concept supplies the groundrules for the calculation of revenues. In assessing financial performance for AP 1, the income side of the Profit and Loss Account does not show the *cash received* in that period but the *income attributable* to sales made in that period, whether the income has been received or not. In our example, 'sales income' in the Profit and Loss (P & L) Account for AP 1 will not represent any inflow of cash whatsoever into the firm in that period. Again, in our example, when the Annual P & L Account is compiled, 'sales income' will represent sales made and cash received for the first eleven periods of the financial year (sales in APs 1–11 with cash received twenty-eight days in arrears) plus sales made in AP 12 for which the cash will be received in AP 1 of the following financial year.

Now, we have seen that financial performance is determined by comparing revenues in a period with expenses. The logic inherent in the realization concept's treatment of revenue must be adhered to in the treatment of expenses. A matching exercise is required. Against the income attributable to a particular period we need to match the expenses incurred in the generation of that income. The accrual concept now takes over.

If we examine the firm's cash outgoings in a particular accounting period, we find a similar pattern to cash inflows: cash outgoings do not necessarily relate to sales generated in the period. If wages are paid one week in arrears, payroll disbursed in Week 1 of AP 1 relates to expenses incurred in generating sales in the last week of the previous AP. A consignment of raw materials may have been paid for in the accounting period but the materials will stay in stock for several periods before being used to generate sales income. Conversely, the raw materials processed in AP 1 were purchased several months before. The firm may have settled its annual rates bill or insurance premiums in the period, expenses which support income generation not for one but for twelve periods. Conversely, resources may have been consumed in the period for which no cash disbursement has yet been made: examples are items billed in arrears, electricity, water, haulage etc.

The accrual concept injects sense and order into this plethora of asymmetrical transactions. In assessing financial performance, the criterion for a legitimate expense is not whether that expense has been settled in cash in the period but whether the expense has been incurred to generate sales in the period. The objective is to establish the cost to the firm of the sales made in the period. So, in respect of the items mentioned above, the P & L Account for AP 1 will contain as an expense payroll costs attributable to the four weeks in the period, despite the fact that payroll for Week 4 will not be disbursed in cash until the first week of AP 2. Only those raw materials used in generating sales income in AP 1 will be charged in the P & L Account as an expense. Where expenses are paid in advance, only that proportion of the expenses which relates to the period is charged: one twelfth of the rates assessment and the insurance premiums will be charged to AP 1. Where goods and services have been consumed in the period but not paid for, the expense of such consumption is assessed and charged in the P & L Account for the period even though no cash has flowed from the firm.

Revenues, then, are matched with expenses in accordance with the logic of the realization and accrual concepts. In this way, the leads and lags which characterize cash transactions are avoided. A genuine measure of financial performance for a particular period is achieved. But, again, it is important to remain sensitive to the specialized nature of the language of finance. Expressions like 'revenues', 'expenses', 'income' and 'cost' are not necessarily synonymous with inflows and outflows of cash. When you examine a P & L Account for a particular period, you are not seeing a record of cash transactions.

The language of finance, then, relies on a syntax which contains seven concepts:

1. Dual aspect
2. Money measurement
3. Business entity
4. Going concern
5. Historical cost
6. Realization
7. Accrual

In addition to these seven concepts, the language contains three major conventions.

1. Consistency convention

'All events of the same character are treated in the same fashion from one period to another.'

In the fast-moving world of the one-minute manager, consistency can be dismissed as a minor virtue. 'All my life,' said Winston Churchill, 'I have had to eat my words and I have found it a most acceptable diet.' In this context the consistency convention can too easily be interpreted as the First Law of Bureaucracy. But, again, it is important to remember that we are dealing with a specialized language: the principle of consistency must be interpreted in its own esoteric context.

The language of finance attempts to bring sense and meaning to complex financial phenomena. We have seen that accountancy is concerned with measurement. In this context, we have even compared the accountant with the surveyor. But the comparison should not be too closely drawn. Measurement, in the financial sense, is not necessarily a science. In some circumstances, it is not subject to natural laws, capable of prediction and clinical verification: nor do these laws apply universally to all instances of the item taken as the object of generalization. Two plus two *does* equal four; the problem lies in assigning the value 'two' to the items needing to be measured. For, in many instances, financial measurement entails valuation rather than counting, judgement rather than reliance on simple arithmetic. Accordingly, financial measurement is not so much a science as an art. Unless principles of consistency are maintained, the art can easily become a black art.

The problems of valuation can be isolated by example. As part of our snapshot of the firm's financial position, we need to place a value on the amounts outstanding to the firm from debtors. Debtors are an asset and the valuation will obviously have an impact on the asset-valuation of the firm.

From outstanding invoices, we calculate that £20m is owed to us by our customers. But past experience has shown that 5 per cent of the total amount outstanding is never, in fact, settled; customers collapse, individuals abscond, quality complaints are made, consignments go astray. As a result, a proportion of debtors represents what, in the jargon, is known as a 'non-performing asset'. In recognition of this, past practice has been to reduce the valuation of outstanding debtors by 5 per cent as a provision for bad debts. The consistency convention determines that this past practice will not be arbitrarily discontinued. In our example, such discontinuation would, at a stroke, increase the asset value of the firm by £1m.

Similar problems apply in the valuation of stocks. Stocks of high-bulk raw materials may be subject to deterioration over time. Techniques will have been developed in the firm to measure such deterioration. Arbitrary departure from such techniques can cause significant financial change. Stocks of semi-finished goods – ships without engines, teapots without spouts, Barbie dolls without knickers – are notoriously difficult to value. But formulae will have been developed. These formulae represent the firm's accumulated experience. It is this experience which the consistency convention reinforces. Without such reinforcement, manipulation becomes easy.

Consider the example of a firm which is replacing a fixed asset like for like. Experience has shown that fixed assets of this type have a useful economic life of five years. The firm is anxious to improve its short-term financial performance as reflected in its P & L Account. In the absence of a consistency convention, the firm could assign a ten-year life to the replacement asset. If the cost of the replacement asset were £1m, depreciation, on the old basis, would be £200k per annum for five years, and on the new basis £100k per annum for ten years. In the short term (years 1–5) the P & L Account would be 'sweetened' and financial performance 'improved' by £100k per annum.

Measurement, then, in the financial sense of valuation, calls for the exercise of reasoned judgement. In a world of imperfectly reasonable men, the consistency of established practice sets a limit to the manipulation of values. Established practices will be set out in the firm's published accounts. Any departures must be similarly publicized and meet with the approval of the firm's auditors. Without the constraint of consistency, in a world of imperfectly reasonable men, the temptation to move down the spiral of manipulation – from 'massaging the figures' to 'cosmetic accounting' to 'creative accounting' to criminal offences with sonorous names (peculation, embezzlement, misappropriation) – would be the greater. Sense would easily be rendered nonsense. In the language of finance, consistency is *not* a minor virtue.

2. Convention of conservatism

'An asset is recorded at the lower of two possible values or an event is recorded in such a way that the owner's equity is lower than it would otherwise have been.'

The essence of the convention is that a known future loss should always be anticipated in the firm's accounts but credit should never be taken now for a profit which has not yet materialized. The convention of conservatism is often cited as proof positive of the accountant's disinclination to look on the bright side of life. But the accountant would tend to agree with George Eliot: 'Nothing is so good as it appears beforehand.' The future, from whichever direction you approach, is usually up-hill and against the wind.

The light at the end of the tunnel is often the headlamp of an approaching express. But, again, these undertones of Victorian gloom make the convention a powerful constraint on manipulation.

To see how the convention operates, let us return to the theme of measurement. The valuation of stocks of finished products provides a good example. How do we value a finished product which, in a matter of days, may be sold and despatched to the customer? If it is in saleroom condition and the market is buoyant, the answer would appear obvious. We should value it at sales price. However, sales price includes an element of profit which has not yet been realized. To value on this basis would be to anticipate a profit which has not yet been secured. In the normal course of events valuation would not be at sales price but at what it has cost the firm to make the product. However, if the market is not buoyant and sale is only feasible at a heavily discounted price, valuation will be made at the lower cost or the discounted price. In this way, a future loss would be anticipated. Valuation, then, is usually struck at the lowest of:

   (i) what it has cost to make the product
  (ii) sales price
 (iii) net realizable value

The onset of recession has brought with it a further application of the convention of conservatism. Many firms, in the process of becoming lean, fit and hungry, have devised corporate plans which involve large-scale redundancies, plant closures and asset disposals spread over a number of future years. Relying on the convention of conservatism, some firms have treated the total cost of such shrinkage as a future cost and charged it against revenue in the P & L Account of the year in which the corporate plan was launched.

British Airways provides a good example. In 1981, BA unveiled its corporate plan. A substantial number of redundancies were envisaged but the programme would take several years to complete. BA's P & L Account for 1981/2 showed an operating surplus of £13m. However, after charging interest and 'extraordinary items', this modest operating surplus was transformed into an overall loss of £544m. 'Extraordinary items' included a sum of £198.8m for 'severance scheme costs'. Of this amount, just over

50 per cent related to severances which took place in 1981/2. The balance (£98.4m) represented the application of the convention of conservatism. The future cost of this aspect of the corporate plan was known at the time. Therefore, it was anticipated in the present and charged in the 1981/2 accounts. Credit for the benefits which would flow from the corporate plan, the unrealized future profit, would not be taken until they actually materialized.

The convention of conservatism sounds a cautionary note and holds optimism, in its extreme forms, in check. It is not a barrier to change. It rather ensures that the case for change must be closely explored before such change is implemented.

3. Convention of materiality

'Immaterial events are disregarded.'

Accountancy, like the law, should not concern itself with trivialities. It has been said that if a mouse ran across a factory floor, the personnel manager would jump on a chair, the plant manager would attempt to strangle it with his bare hands while the accountant would try to count and put a value on it. The convention of materiality precludes the expenditure of undue effort on trivialities. At the financial year-end, scattered throughout the firm are scores of items of low value – pencils, pens, paperclips, notepads etc. They have value but their value is insignificant in determining the firm's financial position and performance. They are immaterial.

The language of finance, then, is a specialized language with its own peculiar syntax. The syntax contains seven concepts and three conventions. The concepts and conventions provide the groundrules by which the language makes sense of complex financial phenomena. The language of finance is not a dead language, the Sanskrit of the managerial world. It can change to reflect altered circumstances. But change is evolutionary, not revolutionary. Great store is placed on tradition and experience. Having examined the territory of finance and its language, we can now turn our attention to the territory's main topographical features.

3. The Topography of the Financial Territory

'Nothing occurs by chance but there is a reason and necessity for everything.'

Leucippus (c. 450 BC)

The landscape of the financial territory is dominated by three major topographical features, the Balance Sheet, the Profit and Loss Account and the Sources and Uses of Funds Statement. We have already seen that each feature performs a different function:

Feature	*Function*
1. Balance Sheet	1. Financial Position
2. Profit and Loss Account	2. Financial Performance
3. Sources and Uses of Funds Statement	3. Liquidity/Cash Flow Measurement

The roots of each feature can be taced to the dynamic cash model of the firm (see Chapter 1). But some disentanglement is required in isolating the separate nature and format of each feature. Let us examine each of the major topographical features in turn.

1. Balance sheet

The balance sheet is a 'financial statement which summarizes, at a particular date, the sources of funds which the firm controls and the ways in which these funds have been used'. If we work from the dynamic cash model (Figure 1), the format of the balance sheet can be derived in three stages:

(i) the components of the model are classified into two categories. The first category comprises those items which bring funds into the firm (sources). The second category incorporates those items which such funds have been used to acquire or support (uses). In the model, funds have been derived from shareholders, retained profits (or 'reserve'), loans (short and long term) and creditors. Some of these items (loans and creditors) represent liabilities, others (shareholders' capital and reserve) represent equities. Funds from these sources have been applied on fixed and current assets. Under the dual aspect these assets will equal the value of liabilities plus equities, and sources will balance with uses.

Sources of Funds	Uses of Funds
Share capital and reserves	Fixed assets
Long-term liabilities (loans)	Current assets
Current liabilities (creditors and short-term loans)	

(ii) Within these two categories ('sources' and 'uses'), the components are ranked in reverse order of liquidity: the component which will be turned into cash the earliest is ranked the last. If we apply such a reverse chronology to the sources of funds, the item which needs to be redeemed the furthest in the future is share capital. By definition, this is the permanent capital of the firm. Long-term liabilities, the semi-permanent capital of the firm, will rank next and current liabilities will rank last. Under 'uses', fixed assets are least easy or likely to be turned into cash while current assets, like debtors, will be encashed within the normal collection period of the firm. The adoption of this specialized chronology produces the following format:

Sources of Funds	Uses of Funds
LONG-TERM	LONG-TERM
Share capital and reserves	Fixed assets
Long-term liabilities	
SHORT-TERM	SHORT-TERM
Current liabilities	Current assets

(iii) Finally, the components are sub-divided into their constituent parts and these constituents are ranked in reverse order of liquidity:

Sources of Funds	**Uses of Funds**
LONG-TERM	LONG-TERM
1. *Share capital and reserves*	4. *Fixed assets*
Share capital	Land and buildings
Reserves	Plant and machinery
2. *Long-term liabilities*	
Loans	
SHORT-TERM	SHORT-TERM
3. *Current liabilities*	5. *Current assets*
Short-term loans	Short-term investments
Overdraft	Raw materials
Creditors	Work-in-progress
	Finished goods
	Debtors
	Cash and bank

This format is usually known as the 'horizontal' method of presentation. More popular these days is the 'vertical' or 'net asset' format which, in the age of convenience, fits more easily into modern paper sizes. The same financial information is presented in both formats at Figure 3. The vertical presentation has the advantage of segregating 'net current assets' (working capital).

BALANCE SHEET
31 December 1985

CONVENTIONAL FORMAT

Sources of funds	£k	£k	Uses of funds	£k
1. Share capital & reserves			4. Fixed assets	120
Share capital	100		5. Current assets	100
Reserves	40			
		140		
2. Long-term liabilities		50		
3. Current liabilities		30		
		220		220

'NET ASSET' FORMAT	£k	£k
1. Share capital & reserves		140
2. Long-term liabilities		50
Capital employed		190
4. Fixed assets		120
5. Current assets	100	
6. LESS current liabilities	30	
Net current assets (or working capital)		70
		190

Figure 3: *Alternative balance sheet presentations*

In interpreting the information presented in Figure 3, remember that it is couched in the specialized language of finance. In particular, under the dual aspect, assets must by definition equal liabilities plus equities. Assume that the item 'current assets' contains a stock of finished product valued, in accordance with the convention of conservatism, at what it has cost to produce that stock. We withdraw from stock finished product valued at £10k. We sell the finished product for £12k on twenty-eight days' credit. The effect on the balance sheet is as follows:

Sources of Funds		Uses of Funds	
SHARE CAPITAL & RESERVES	£k	CURRENT ASSETS	£k
Reserve (retained profit)	(+)2	Finished goods	(−)10
		Debtors	(+)12
	(+)2		(+) 2

In other words, the two sides will balance at a higher level, both capital employed and net assets increase to the extent of the profit on the transaction. The balance is maintained when the debtor duly settles. On the 'uses' side, debtors are reduced by £12k and cash is increased by the same amount.

But remember that the balance sheet is a static analysis of a dynamic process. The information appertains to a single date only. If the firm is prone to seasonal factors, the balance sheet at the year end will reflect a particular point in this cycle of seasonality and may not present a representative picture of the firm's financial position.

2. Profit and Loss Account

Whereas the balance sheet is concerned with the financial position of the firm, assets and liabilities, at one point in time, the P & L Account concentrates on financial performance, revenues in comparison with expenses, over a period of time. The terms 'revenues' and 'expenses' are used in the specialized sense assigned by the realization and accrual concepts:

'revenues': amounts received or due to be received for goods sold/services rendered during the accounting period;

'expenses': what it has cost the firm to produce the goods sold or to provide the services rendered in order to generate the revenues indicated.

Such specialized usage enables revenues to be matched with expenses over a given period of time.

Within the firm, the P & L Account forms the centre-piece of the management information system. It is also the headline item in the firm's Published Accounts. Internal (or Management) Accounts and Published Accounts are conditioned by the same specialized language of finance but serve different purposes. The focus of the former is the internal management of the firm, the monitoring and control of performance. As such, internal accounts will be highly detailed in terms of revenues and expenses and capable of disaggregation into the major activities of the firm. Published Accounts, duly certified by external auditors, provide the means whereby management renders account to the shareholders for its stewardship of their assets. In these accounts, turnover (sales revenue) and trading profit must be shown but there is no legal obligation to disclose details of expenses. Quite apart from 'stewardship', Published Accounts in recent years have become yet another component of a firm's public relations mission. Gone are the days when Published Accounts were presented, sparse and spare, between sombre, fustian covers. Annual accounts now come in psychedelic hues, packed with photographs, artists' impressions and histograms. Companies have even produced accounts in the shape of their products. All that remains to be produced is the first full-frontal, pop-up *Book of Accounts*. But whatever the exotica, the Management Accounts must reconcile with the Published Accounts.

A typical format, in summarized form, for a manufacturing concern, from Management to Published Accounts, is shown below:

MANAGEMENT ACCOUNTS	
Profit and Loss Account £k	*12 months to 31 Dec. 1985*
Sales 150	Amounts received or to be received for goods sold during the accounting year
LESS Cost of goods sold 100	The 'direct' costs incurred by the firm in the production of the goods sold in the accounting year – operatives' wages, materials consumed, factory overheads etc
Gross profit 50	
LESS Overhead 20	Administrative (personnel, finance dept, etc.) and selling expenses
Trading or operating profit 30	

In a retail firm, cost of goods sold would comprise the purchase price of the merchandize sold. In this context 'gross profit' is usually styled 'gross margin'. In all activities, 'cost of goods sold' and 'overhead' would be disaggregated into main expense items.

Sales (turnover) and operating (trading) profit now dovetail into the format required for Published Accounts.

PUBLISHED ACCOUNTS		
Profit and Loss Account	£k	*12 months to 31 Dec. 1985*
Sales (Turnover)	150	
Trading profit for the year	30	
LESS Interest	1	Interest paid or payable on borrowings for the 12-month period
Profit before tax	29	
LESS Corporation tax	12	Tax liability on 12 months' results
Net profit for year after tax	17	

In the Published Accounts, the Profit and Loss Account now leads into the Appropriation Account.

Appropriation Account	£k	*12 months to 31 Dec. 1985*
Net profit for year after tax	17	
LESS Ordinary Dividend	5	Amount payable to ordinary shareholders
Retained from year's profit	12	
ADD Unappropriated balance ('reserve') brought forward from last year-end	22	'Reserve', or total profits retained in business since its inception, at end of previous financial year
Unappropriated balance carried forward	34	'Reserve' in balance sheet at 31 December 1985

It will be noted that the Published Accounts contain four items which, in some form, carry the designation 'profit' – trading profit (£30k), profit before tax (£29k), profit after tax (£17k) and retained profit (£12k). Beware statements of profit which carry no precise definition. The two most quoted 'profits' are trading profit (profit before interest and tax) and profit before tax. If the firm has high borrowings and hefty interest payments, the quotation of trading profit in isolation will put a roseate hue on financial performance and prove yet again that it is possible to tell the truth and nothing but the truth without actually telling the whole truth.

The balance sheet and the Profit and Loss Account share common roots in the dynamic cash model of the firm. They reflect different perspectives on the same set of phenomena, the former encompassing financial position, the latter financial performance. As a result of this common root-stock, there are major linkages between the two.

Some of these linkages are straightforward. The change in reserves between one balance sheet and the next represents the retained profit in the Appropriation Account. Interest shown in the P & L Account indicates the cost to the firm of the borrowings shown in the balance sheet. Similarly the tax and dividend shown in the P & L Account will appear as current liabilities in the balance sheet, to be disbursed to the Inland Revenue and the shareholders at some future date beyond the financial year-end.

Other linkages are less apparent. The balance sheet is concerned with assets and liabilities, the P & L Account with revenues and expenses. For a manufacturing concern, the balance sheet will show, under current assets, the value of stocks of raw material at the year end. The value of such stocks at the start of the year will be shown in the previous year's balance sheet. The focus of the P & L Account is different. It needs to show, as an expense, that level of raw material consumption which was experienced in generating annual sales revenue. Some of this raw material may have been drawn from stocks in place at the end of the previous financial year; some may have been purchased and consumed in the same financial year; some may have been purchased in the financial year in question, but remain unconsumed at the year end. Within the firm, invoices and other records will show amounts purchased and prices paid. The amount of raw materials consumed in the financial year can be calculated from the formula:

consumption = opening stock (+) purchases (−) closing stock

All the time stocks are being withdrawn, consumed in the production process and duly charged as an expense in the P & L Account. Simultaneously stocks are being replenished with new deliveries from suppliers. The materials are stocked not necessarily for withdrawal in chronological order but for ease of handling and to meet space constraints. Physical quantities received from suppliers and checked out to production are readily identifiable. The difficulty arises in placing a financial value on these physical amounts consumed in generating sales revenue.

Assume that the firm is planning to start production of a new line in April 1985. The new line incorporates a component which is bought in from several sources of supply. Stocks of the component are built up as follows in advance of the start of production:

Delivered	*No.*	*Price per Component*	*Total Cost*
		£	£
9 January 1985	1,000	2.75	2,750
14 February 1985	2,000	3.50	7,000
20 March 1985	3,000	3.75	11,250
End March 1985	6,000		21,000

If the balance sheet were struck at the end of March 1985, it would record, as a current asset, the stock of components valued, in accordance with the historical cost concept, at £21k. In April 1985, production duly starts. Two thousand components are withdrawn from stock in the April accounting period and incorporated into the new products, all of which are sold and despatched to customers. But at what value are these two thousand components to be charged to the P & L Account as an appropriate expense against sales revenue generated in the April accounting period? A number of approaches are possible:

a. *First in, first out (FIFO)*

Although the components are homogeneous and are physically stocked not in order of receipt but to facilitate efficient distribution, the FIFO method assigns a notional chronology to the stocks. It assumes that those stocks which are received the earliest will be used the first in the production process. So in our example, the two thousand components are charged to the April P & L Account at:

Delivered	No.	Price £	Total Cost £
January 1985	1,000	2.75	2,750
February 1985	1,000	3.50	3,500
	2,000		6,250

And, at the end of April, assuming no further purchases, the remaining components will be valued in the balance sheet at £14,750:

Delivered	No.	Price £	Total Cost £
February 1985	1,000	3.50	3,500
March 1985	3,000	3.75	11,250
	4,000		14,750

b. *Average cost*

Under the average cost method, the average cost of the total stock at the time of withdrawals is calculated. This average cost forms the basis for the charge to the P & L Account and for the valuation of the stocks in the balance sheet. So, in our example, two thousand components are charged to the April P & L Account at an average cost of £3.50, an amount of £7,000. At the end of April, with no further purchases, the remaining components will be valued at £14,000:

	No.	Average Cost £	Valuation £
Stocks at end March 1985	6,000	3.50	21,000
LESS Withdrawals in April 1985	2,000	3.50	7,000
Stocks at end March 1985	4,000	3.50	14,000

On the next delivery of components, the average cost of total stock, including that delivery, would be recalculated. The new average would form the basis for charging when components were next withdrawn from stock and used in the production process.

c. *Last in, first out (LIFO)*

LIFO represents the obverse of FIFO. A reverse chronology is applied: the last consignment received is the first to be charged. So, in our example, the two thousand components are assumed to be drawn from the delivery made on 20 March 1985. They are charged at a cost of £3.75, an amount of £7,500. At the end of April, the remaining components will be valued at £13,500:

Delivery	No.	Price £	Valuation £
January 1985	1,000	2.75	2,750
February 1985	2,000	3.50	7,000
March 1985	1,000	3.75	3,750
	4,000		13,500

In physical terms, the three methods, FIFO, Average Cost and LIFO, summarize the same events. But the results are markedly different:

Method	Cost of Components in P & L Account (April 1985) £	Balance Sheet Valuation of Components (April 1985) £
FIFO	6,250	14,750
Average Cost	7,000	14,000
LIFO	7,500	13,500

For the April accounting period, LIFO produces material costs 20 per cent higher than FIFO. None of the methods infringe the historical cost convention; all are based on the acquisition cost of the components. The method adopted will be described in a note to the balance sheet in the firm's Published Accounts. Obviously the convention of consistency precludes frequent changes of method: the problems of stock valuation have been accentuated by high levels of inflation. These problems are discussed in Chapter 10.

In most companies, fixed assets are a key factor in the generation of sales revenue. If we take a machine as an example, the written-down value is recorded in the balance sheet. The P & L Account picks up as expenses the wages of the machine operators, the cost of materials processed by the machine, the machine's power costs etc. But how do we make a charge for the fixed asset itself? The fixed asset, obviously, has contributed greatly to the generation of revenue but how is the charge for this contribution to be assessed? How can a long-term capital item like a machine be expressed in a revenue account?

Assume that we purchase a machine for £100k at the start of 1986. We take into account experience with similar assets and assess the machine's useful economic life at five years. We purchase the machine on three months' credit and settle, in cash, at the end of March, 1986. £100k in cash duly flows out of the firm. The machine is utilized at full capacity throughout the year. The machine has been crucial to the generation of sales revenue in 1986. But we cannot represent the expense of this contribution by charging the purchase price of the machine to the P & L Account for 1986. £100k in cash has certainly departed from the firm in respect of the machine in 1986 but, under the accrual concept, profit or loss is not derived from the difference between cash receipts and cash disbursements in the financial year. For if we did charge the £100k as an expense against sales revenue in 1986, we would have a mismatch. Given that we anticipate a five-year life for the machine, if we charged the purchase price in its entirety for 1986, we would be charging against one year's sales revenue the expense of five years' revenue generation from that machine.

As we have seen, the process of depreciation is designed to overcome these problems. Through this process, the capital cost of the fixed asset is gradually transformed as an expense to the P & L Account throughout the useful economic life of the asset. The 'straight-line' method provides the easiest and most common way of calculating an appropriate annual depreciation charge. The historical cost of the asset is divided by the asset's estimated useful life to produce the depreciation chargeable to the P & L Account in each year of that useful life. In our example:

$$\frac{\text{historical cost}}{\text{useful economic life}} = \frac{£100k}{5} = £20k \text{ p.a. for five years}$$

This particular asset has a depreciation rate of 20 per cent on historical cost. The 'expensing' of the fixed asset through the P & L Account at £20k p.a. is reflected in the balance sheet by 'writing down' the value of the asset. In the balance sheets at the year-end of 1986 and 1987, the asset will be valued as follows:

Fixed asset: machine	1986	1987
	£k	£k
Gross value (historical cost)	100	100
LESS accumulated depreciation	20	40
Written-down (or 'net book') value (WDV or NBV)	80	60

In each of the two years, £20k will have been charged as an expense ('depreciation') in the P & L Account.

Remember that the written-down value of an asset does not represent either the re-sale value or the replacement cost of that asset. WDV is simply the end product of a highly specialized formula derived from the language of finance. Remember also that 'straight-line' depreciation is charged in full in the P & L Account even if the asset is only partially utilized. Depreciation is a function of time not capacity utilization. If fixed assets are being consistently under-utilized, depreciation is the financial equivalent of feeding hay to a dead horse.

Sources and Uses of Funds Statement

The balance sheet provides a static analysis at one particular date of the sources of a firm's funds and the uses to which these funds have been applied. The Sources and Uses of Funds Statement adds an element of dynamism. Again the Statement's roots lie in the dynamic cash model of the firm and it draws from both the balance sheet and the P & L Account. But its purpose is quite distinct. It is concerned with neither financial position nor financial performance but with changes over time in terms of the sources of funds available to the firm and the disposition of such funds within the firm. The Statement contains within itself the 'cash flow' of the firm.

In format, the Statement starts with changes in the funds available to the firm within a defined time span. Such changes will have emanated from three sources:

(a) *Profit and Loss Account*

We have seen that retained profit (profit after the deduction of interest, tax and dividend) represents an increase in shareholders' equity which is available for re-investment in the firm. However, retained profit understates funds available from internal sources. Profit is calculated as the difference between revenue and appropriate expenses. These expenses include a charge for depreciation. But as we have seen, depreciation, unlike wages, materials, salaries, rent, etc., does not represent an outflow of cash from the firm. Rather it represents the recovery over an asset's useful life of previous capital expenditure and past cash outflows. Such capital expenditure is accommodated, as we shall see, as a use of funds. Hence, in quantifying sources of funds generated by internal operations, depreciation needs to be excluded from the expenses charged in the P & L Account. The easiest way to achieve this is simply to add the depreciation charge back on to the retained profit:

funds from internal operations = retained profit (+) depreciation.

(b) *Balance sheet, liability and equity items*

An increase in these items (excluding retained profit at (a) above) between two balance sheet dates provides a source of additional funds. A new issue of shares or increased borrowing brings new funds into the firm. Less obviously, an increase in creditors produces the same result.

(c) *Balance sheet, asset items*

A decrease in these items provides the firm with additional funds. Disposal of a fixed asset, such as the sale of plant, land or buildings, brings funds into the firm. Similarly, a reduction of the cash tied up in stock and debtors liberates funds for alternative uses.

Having analyzed the sources, the Statement then concentrates on how the funds generated from these sources have been used. Funds have been used if:

(a) *Profit and Loss Account*

The firm has incurred a loss (after interest, tax and dividend) and the loss is greater than the depreciation charge.

(b) *Balance sheet*

There has been a decrease (excluding (a) above) in liability and equity items: if borrowings or creditors have diminished, funds have been applied from some other source to offset this decrease.

(c) *Balance sheet*

There has been an increase in asset items: capital expenditure will be reflected in the increased gross value of fixed assets: increase in stocks and debtors will absorb additional funds.

The mechanics of the generation and absorption of funds can be summarized in terms of the model at Figure 4:

Item	Source	Use
P & L (+) depreciation	Positive	Negative
Liabilities & equities	Increase	Decrease
Assets	Decrease	Increase

Figure 4: *Movement of funds*

From the analysis flows the format of the Statement:

Sources of funds	£
Profit	x
Depreciation	x
Increases in liability/equity items*	x
Decreases in asset items	x
	—
	x
	—

Uses of funds	
Loss	x
Increases in asset items	x
Decreases in liability items	x
	—
	x
	—

*Exclude increase in reserves, picked up from P & L Account.

In accordance with the dual aspect, sources will equal uses. If, for example, the firm had generated funds by increasing its borrowings, this source would have been applied in increasing asset items (fixed or current) or in offsetting the effect of decreases in other liability items (creditors). For every source, there is a use.

To put theory into practice, a firm's balance sheets for years ending 31 December 1985 and 1986 are shown at Figure 5.

A Sources and Uses of Funds Statement is then derived from this data.

	31 Dec. 1985		31 Dec. 1986	
1. *Shareholders' funds*	£k	£k	£k	£k
60,000 ordinary shares	60		60	
Reserves	22		34	
		82		94
2. *Long-term loans*		20		20
Capital employed		102		114
3. *Fixed assets*				
Gross	60		70	
LESS Accumulated depreciation	18		24	
Written-down value		42		46
4. *Net current assets*				
Stocks	60		70	
Debtors	30		40	
Cash and bank	10		8	
LESS Creditors	(40)	60	(50)	68
Net assets		102		114

Figure 5: *Balance sheets, years ending 1985 and 1986*

In drawing up the Statement, look first for the sources of funds. Reserves have increased by £12k. Cross reference to the Appropriation Account will confirm that retained profits of £12k were attributable to 1986. In striking this profit, depreciation has been charged as an expense; this must be added back to the retained profit. The relevant amount is £6k, the figure by which accumulated depreciation has increased in 1986. Access to the detailed P & L Account would confirm this figure. Creditors have increased from £40k to £50k thereby providing the firm with additional funds of £10k. An asset item, cash and bank has decreased by £2k, releasing funds for use elsewhere. In total an additional £30k of funds has become available to the firm. How has it been applied? Three asset items, fixed assets (gross), stocks and debtors have each absorbed an additional £10k of funds. The Sources and Uses of Funds Statement is shown in Figure 6:

Sources of funds	£k
Rotained profits	12
Depreciation	6
Increased creditors	10
Cash and bank	2
	30
Uses of funds	
Increases in fixed assets	10
Increases in stocks	10
Increase in debtors	10
	30

Figure 6: *Sources and Uses of Funds Statement*

Again a caveat must be entered on seasonality. The Statement is derived from the financial position at two precise dates. It is easy to reach the assumption that the changes have occurred smoothly and gradually over the intervening period. In fact, in a highly seasonal firm, short-term borrowings may well have been required to finance stocks in the trough of the sales graph. Such short-term fluctuations will slip beneath the radar of the Sources and Uses of Funds Statement based on two year-end dates.

Having examined the ground-plan of the territory of finance, made passing acquaintance with its language and cast our eyes over its main topographical features, we must now address a fundamental question. How is this territory to be managed?

4. Managing the Financial Territory

'There are only two problems in Life: deciding what to do and doing it.'

Anon.

The above philosophy, from the School of the Positive Mental Attitudinalists via a Christmas cracker, while true, can hardly claim to be an exhaustive description of the subtle processes of human existence. However, the philosophy does capture the essential requirements for effective management of the financial territory. Objectives need to be determined and systems established whereby people in the organization can monitor and control progress towards the objectives.

The method by which objectives are determined will be influenced by the political system of the firm. However, once definite objectives begin to emerge, they translate into the language of finance as the answers to two questions:

  (i) What, in financial terms, does the firm want to do?
  (ii) How is the firm to provide the funds to do it?

As we shall see, the answers can start up an iterative process. We know what we want to do but the funds are not available to do it. Hence objectives need to be scaled down or the period for their realization extended. But will funds be available for these more modest ambitions? And so on, until a match is achieved. When such a match has been made, appropriate systems will be required to monitor and control progress. We consider first the objective-setting process, then the design of appropriate systems.

The static analysis of the balance sheet, in its 'vertical' format (Figure 5) portrays the firm in a state of financial equilibrium. This equilibrium reflects a situation wherein:

shareholders' funds (+) long-term loans =
fixed assets (+) working capital

But 'equilibrium' is used in a descriptive rather than an evaluative sense. There is no particular merit in having a balance sheet which balances. The tautology is the same whatever the language. What matters is not *that* balance is achieved but *how* balance is achieved. For example, equilibrium may rest on a potentially ruinous Everest of borrowings used to acquire a set of under- and non-performing assets. 'Equilibrium', then, is used in the specialized context of the 'dual aspect'. The Sources and Uses of Funds Statement represents another species of equilibrium analysis. The statement, as we have seen, shows the funds which become available to the firm in a defined period and the uses which the firm has made of these funds. In this analysis there are four variables:

(i)   retained profit (or loss) (+) depreciation (internal funding, if positive)
(ii) changes in share capital or borrowings (external funding)
(iii) changes in working capital
(iv) changes in fixed assets (capital expenditure)

In the example at Figure 6:

(i)   retained profit (+) depreciation amounted to £18,000
(ii) there were no changes in share capital or borrowings
(iii) working capital increased by £8,000 ((increase in stocks (+) increase in debtors) minus (increase in creditors (+) reduction in cash and bank))
(iv) Capital expenditure amounted to £10,000 (increase in gross fixed assets)

These changes are depicted in the form of an equilibrium model at Figure 7.

In this example, *past* changes are analyzed. The model can also be used to analyze *future* planned changes and, in this context, is particularly useful in considering answers to the two fundamental questions of the objective-setting process:

(i) What, in financial terms, does the firm want to do?
(ii) How is the firm to provide the funds to do it?

Let us assume that we are dealing with a firm which, in financial terms, is currently successful. It has expanded and wants to go on expanding. It has translated its expansionary ambitions into a set of precisely quantified marketing objectives. But such expansion will be capital-intensive. Funds will be required for investment in additional fixed assets. Such an increase in fixed assets entails additional working capital. A greater or more varied volume of sales and output will usually require more funds to be tied up in debtors or stocks unless longer lines of credit can be extracted from suppliers. In brief, to achieve its expansionary objectives, the firm will require a greater availability of funds.

Let us assume that what the firm wants to do will require in the next financial year capital expenditure of £20m and additional working capital of £5m. So how is the firm to provide the funds to achieve these objectives? Retained profit and depreciation in the same period is estimated to produce £12m. The resulting 'disequilibrium' model is shown at Figure 8.

From the model, it will be seen that equilibrium can only be achieved if the funding gap of £13m can be bridged. Otherwise the objectives will need to be scaled down. The corporate head is now scratched. Facts are assimilated, value judgements made and the political process begins to operate. The environment is not suited to a further issue of shares. Borrowings are already heavy and interest rates high: further indebtedness will simply heap Ossa upon Pelion. So, if the opportunity of bridging the gap through an infusion of external funds is not feasible, solutions must be sought from the other three variables – retained profit (+) depreciation, working capital, and capital expenditure (fixed assets). So:

(i) Can the firm increase internally generated funds by a mixture of revenue enhancement and cost reduction?
(ii) Can the additional working capital requirement be

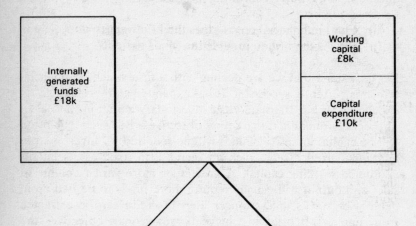

Figure 7: *Equilibrium model*

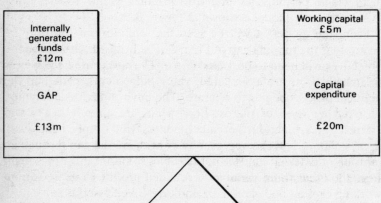

Figure 8: *Disequilibrium model*

reduced by sweating longer lines of credit out of suppliers, by scaling down stockholdings, by tightening credit extended to customers?

(iii) Can items in the capital expenditure programme be deleted or deferred without drastically altering the direction in which the firm wishes to go?

As these questions are discussed and answers emerge, the model can be manipulated. The firm decides that, with a major cost reduction exercise, internally generated funds can be increased by £2m. Additional working capital can be contained at £2m. Items in the capital expenditure programme to the extent of £5m can be deferred. The gap is reduced to £3m. The firm decides that, despite the level of interest rates, this gap can be bridged by an increase in borrowings. Equilibrium is restored. (Figure 9.)

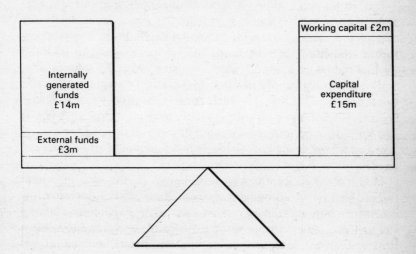

Figure 9: *Equilibrium restored*

The equilibrium model provides a means of sub-dividing the financial territory into a series of manageable administrative regions. Each of the four variables in the model constitutes a focus of managerial attention:

Variable	Focus
(i) Internally generated funds	Management of the P & L Account
(ii) Working capital	Cash management
(iii) Capital expenditure	Asset management
(iv) External funding	Management of the capital structure

We shall examine in subsequent chapters specific techniques for the effective management of each of the four regions. Inter-regional relationships, the linkages between the variables, will also need to be managed. And, like all nation states, the territory of finance is greater than the sum of its parts. Overall direction and control will be required to guide the regions towards the national objectives.

But, in planning future strategy, from which side of the model does the firm start? Does it start from the uses side, calculate the cost of the strategy in terms of capital expenditure and working capital and hope that the funds will be forthcoming to take the waiting out of its wanting? Or does it start from the sources side, work out its availability of funds and cut its strategic coat to this financial cloth? Does it start from the proclivity to spend (permissive society) or from the ability to pay (Victorian virtues)? We have strayed into the Great Political Debate of Our Times. Are you a 'wet' (proclivity to spend)? Or are you a 'dry' (ability to pay)?

Classical financial theory, formulated in the era of sound finance and balanced budgets, favours the approach with the low moisture content. 'Finance must determine expenditure', is its rallying cry. Internally generated funds must determine what a firm can afford to spend on capital equipment and additional working capital. Classical theory does not preclude additional borrowings but seeks to limit the amount by the application of a high 'self-financing' ratio. The 'self-financing ratio' represents that proportion of capital expenditure which a firm should meet from internally generated funds. So, if a firm is working to a self-financing ratio of 80 per cent, internally generated funds of £8m will set a ceiling of £10m on capital expenditure. Classical theory also counsels on the type of capital expenditure for which it is appropriate to borrow. Capital expenditure designed to replace existing assets should be met in its entirety from internally generated funds. The notion is close to much modern conservationist philosophy. Current generations of customers should pay, through the price of the product, to maintain intact that proportion of the firm's fixed assets which is being eroded to satisfy their needs. The bill should not be deferred for posterity to settle. To which the macho manager would respond, 'What's posterity ever done for me?'

Under classical theory, the left-hand side of the model, particularly the amount of internally generated funds, determines the right-hand side. Borrowing is not precluded but carefully controlled in terms of amount and purpose. As we shall see, a high self-financing ratio is reinforced by a lower 'gearing' or 'leverage' (ratio of borrowings to total capital employed).

Most firms would claim to subscribe to classical theory, but statements, policies and beliefs like . . .

- 'you don't hit the jackpot unless you put money in the machine'
- 'our workforce must be the highest-paid on the industry'
- 'we must maintain our engineering leadership'
- 'the capital expenditure programme is sacrosanct'

. . . come close to embracing a revisionist theory in which expenditure is pre-determined and funds must be made available to meet it. Some firms have little option but revisionism. A firm embarks on an ambitious capital programme when its internal generation of funds is high. But the programme will take several years to fructify. Before completion, internal generation starts to falter. If the firm is to complete its programme, borrowings will be necessary at precisely the time when its ability to pay interest is declining. Does the firm stick, twist or bust? If the firm presses on and the capital programme pays off, internally generated funds resume their flow and further capital investment is facilitated. But if the pay-off from the programme is, in financial terms, a concrete parachute, the firm is left to face the oncoming avalanche of its

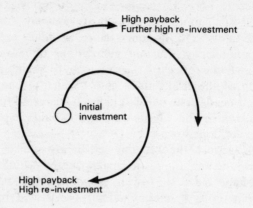

Figure 10: *Japan Incorporated: virtuous circle*

accumulated debts. If it pays off, the investment is the firm's stairway to the stars. If it fails, the firm is left clinging to the wreckage.

In the UK, the 1970s and early 1980s were the era of slow, low or no growth. But growth, at both the macro-level of the state and the micro-level of the firm, remains the major objective of economic activity. The word itself is the *sine qua non* of both political manifestoes and annual reports. Through the process of generating and applying funds, the firm, like the state, is seeking to break into a 'virtuous circle'. Investment leads to high internal generation of funds; these funds are re-invested to produce even higher internal generation, and onwards and upwards we go – the Japan Incorporated Syndrome. (Figure 10.)

What the firm, like the state, is trying to avoid is the 'vicious circle'. Here, initial investment produces a disappointing pay-back and low internal generation of funds. This leads to low investment and even lower internal generation. After much philosophical discussion on whether low investment results from low productivity or vice versa, the firm will finish up chomping on its own tail. The process has been described as '*la maladie Anglaise*'. (Figure 11.)

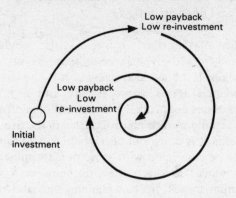

Figure 11: *La maladie Anglaise: vicious circle*

But entry to the 'virtuous circle' can be a long time a-coming. In 1938, Chester F. Carlson, after much research, produced a prototype 'electrophotographic' machine. But turning the prototype into a commercial product drained Carlson's resources and he joined forces with the Batelle Institute. In 1946, the Haloid Corporation acquired the rights to the process and the quest for the commercial model continued. In 1955 Haloid acquired the patent. Between 1947 and 1960, Haloid invested in the process an amount equal to twice its retained profits. At last, in 1960, Haloid hit the motherlode. Xerography was launched on a grateful world and Haloid changed its name to Xerox. In the next decade the value of Xerox's ordinary shares increased by a factor of sixty. Similarly, entry to the 'vicious circle' is not necessarily sudden and through a trap-door. The collapse of many major British industries in recent years can, in many cases, be traced back to a process of erosion spanning two decades.

In managing the financial territory, then, the firm needs to set its objectives. It needs to resolve where it is going and how, in financial terms, it intends to get there. In this objective-setting process, the equilibrium model is useful in testing alternatives and identifying funding gaps. But once the corporate ends have been resolved and the financial means determined, the need then is for systems to enable people in the organization to monitor and control physical and financial progress.

Most accountants, if described as sociologists, would consult a good libel lawyer. However, accountancy, as an academic discipline, can claim to be a social science. It is the discipline of measuring, in financial terms, social activity. But such measurement, in isolation, does not provide the element of control implicit in the word 'management'. For control purposes the firm needs to know not only what it *is* doing but also what it *ought* to be doing. 'Actuals' need to be compared with some predetermined level of intended performance. In brief, the firm requires a means of making such comparisons. It needs a planning and control system.

Appropriate systems rarely come off the peg; they need 'customizing' to fit the peculiar quirks and contours of the individual firm. At the 'hard' end of the specification, firms differ in such factors as size, complexity, product diversity, external environment, time-horizon and organizational structure. At the 'soft' end, style, culture and philosophy range from the sombre to the bizarre. Within the same firm, sharp differences can exist between divisions and locations in both 'hard' and 'soft' factors. The political tendency within the firm will also be a shaping influence. Where power is widely diffused, open access systems will prevail. Where power is concentrated in few people or a dominant ideology, systems will be more *dirigiste*. So the architecture of planning and control systems has infinite possibilities, from Baroque to Bauhaus. But within this architectural range, the building materials of planning and control systems are relatively uniform. Take as an example a firm with a three-tier organizational structure (Figure 12).

Within this organizational shape, decisions need to be made and actions taken at three conceptual levels:

(i) at the level of corporate objectives: the resources required to achieve the objectives must be identified and the allocation of these resources within the firm must be determined

(ii) at the level of physically acquiring the allocated resources at points within the firm and ensuring that the resources

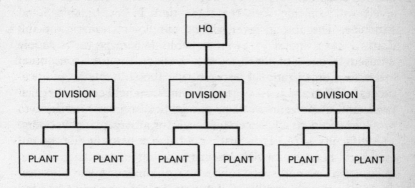

Figure 12: *Three-tier organizational structure*

are efficiently and effectively utilized for the purpose allocated
(iii) at the level of operations, carrying out specific tasks and performing particular functions

The poetry of the process lies in the overlaps between the different conceptual levels. And the form of this poetry, metaphysical, comic or epic, will be influenced by the dominant political tendency within the firm. Where power is concentrated in one individual, the three conceptual levels could represent the three tiers in the organizational structure, king, nobles and vassals. Overlaps may be created but it can be a risky business: '. . . if any man or woman goes to the King inside the inner court without being called, there is but one law: all alike are to be put to death except the one to whom the King holds out the golden sceptre that he may live' (*Esther IV, ii*).

Where power resides in a group of people, there may be inbuilt overlaps between the first two conceptual levels with divisional heads enjoying membership of the seignorial oligarchy. Elsewhere overlaps may be created by the formation of patron-client relationships. Where power is vested in an ideology, the scope for overlaps is limited. Decisions and actions must conform to the ideological blueprint and the blueprint may hermetically seal the three conceptual levels from each other. The three conceptual levels will coincide with the three tiers in the organizational structure. The second level will be purely functionary and the third, as far as possible, programmable. Where power is widely diffused throughout the firm, the overlaps between conceptual levels and organizational tiers provide the stuff of the political process. For there is no necessary symmetry between conceptual levels and organizational tiers. The political process, if effective, provides access to all conceptual levels for all organizational tiers. The difficulty here lies in striking a balance between liberty and efficiency, between the tight control of resources and the provision of sufficient air and space to encourage innovation and unorthodoxy. It is the old conflict of determinism and free will. And the ideal balance can prove as illusory as the ideal male/female relationship – platonic with sex.

Whatever system of planning and control is adopted to manage the financial territory, it will have inherent limitations. The system will produce financial information on quantifiable phenomena. It will not reveal the 'non dollar' variables – the morale of the workforce, the satisfaction of the customer, the machinations of the competitor. Where quantification is possible, the system will show what we are doing and how this compares with what we planned to be doing. It will not show, in the 'softer' areas, what we are not doing and ought, with advantage, to be doing.

Having cleared some philosophical undergrowth and viewed sundry blinding glimpses of the obvious, it is time to examine management in each of the financial territory's major regions – the Profit and Loss Account (internal generation of funds), working capital, capital structure (external funds) and capital expenditure (fixed assets).

5. Managing the Profit and Loss Account

'How can anyone govern a country that has 246 different kinds of cheese?'

Charles de Gaulle

The Profit and Loss Account is concerned with financial performance over a defined period. Financial performance is measured as the difference between revenues and expenses. As we have seen, revenues and expenses are not synonymous with cash inflows and outflows in the relevant period. Revenues relate to the sales attributable to the period while expenses reflect the cost of making sales. But in attempting to manage the revenues and expenses of the large, modern firm we are confronted, like Charles de Gaulle, with the problem of fashioning order out of diversity. For, in the era of corporate giganticism, the firm can be multinational, multi-product and multi-locational and contain within its organizational structure a multiplicity of complex financial interrelationships. The global revenues and expenses of the firm may be discernible with relative ease. The difficulty lies in arranging an appropriate disaggregation of these totals so that the financial performance of the firm's constituent activities can be assessed with some accuracy. Without such disaggregation, we are trying to monitor and control the whole but not the parts, the effects but not the causes.

As an example of the difficulties of disaggregation, take a manufacturing firm with diverse product lines. The firm has a three-tier organizational structure – headquarters, division, plant. Within the firm, there are thirty manufacturing plants grouped into four divisions. Headquarters, divisions and plants are located at geographically separate sites. In addition, the firm has an in-house Research and Development Centre and a central computer resource. Consider just some of the complexities in managing the firm's P & L Account.

First, on the revenue side, there is no major problem in assembling the firm's total revenue for a particular period. Difficulties arise when it is attempted to disaggregate this total revenue among the four divisions and thirty manufacturing plants. Assume an element of vertical integration in the firm: Plant A in Division 1 makes a component which is not sold 'at arm's length' to an external customer but is transferred to Plant B in Division 2 for incorporation into Plant B's product, which is duly sold on a commercial basis to third parties. How do we value the transfer of the component from Plant A to Plant B? What figure will appear in Plant A's P & L Account as revenue and in Plant B's as expense? The ultimate price paid by the customer for the final product is known, but what proportion is attributable to Plant A and Plant B? The transfer could be valued at what it had cost Plant A to make the component or at what it would cost Plant B to acquire the component from outside the firm. Or some compromise could be essayed which added a 'mark-up' to cost. There is no 'correct' answer but the different approaches produce significantly different assessments of the financial performance of the two plants.

Secondly, on the expenses side, the thirty plants are generating revenues and incurring expenses at plant level. But, apart from such localized expenditure, expenses are also being incurred at divisional and headquarters level without the generation of material revenues. These expenses, however tenuous the link, are being incurred *on behalf of* the plants but not directly *by* the plants. Obviously, any matching of revenues and expenses at plant level needs to recognize such 'overhead' expenditure if an accurate assessment of financial performance is to be made. But on what basis should such overhead expenditure be allocated to individual plants?

If the Profit and Loss Account is to be effectively managed, there needs to be created from a potential jungle of issues an ordered landscape. This landscape needs to contain two essential characteristics:

   (i) the characteristic of measurability: the financial per-
       formance of the constituent activities in the firm must be
       capable of separate quantification
  (ii) the characteristic of accountability: the responsibility
       for financial performance at various levels within these
       constituent activities must be capable of allocation to
       individuals

The first task, then, in the effective management of the P & L
Account is organizational. An appropriate landscape needs to be
created.

The most common approaches to the creation of this landscape lie
through:

   (i) cost centres
  (ii) contribution centres
 (iii) profit centres

Each approach provides a different assessment of the 'financial
performance' of the constituent activities within the firm. The
three are considered below.

1. Cost centre approach

The complexities of disaggregating revenues and expenses are
avoided by being ignored. Revenue remains a global total for the
firm as a whole. The focus of measurement and accountability is
set firmly on expenses. Each discrete activity (HQ, Division,
R & D Centre, Computer Resource) and each location (plant) is
categorized as a cost centre. To each cost centre are charged those
expenses directly incurred by that centre. In this way, all activities
and locations within the firm, whether revenue-generating or not,
are treated the same. The Profit and Loss Account for the firm is,
quite simply, the global revenue for the firm as a whole matched
with the aggregation of each cost centre's expenses for the relevant
period.

The cost centre approach has the advantage of simplicity. The
exclusion of revenue as a control factor may also reflect reality if

marketing is a centralized activity and production simply reflects central decisions on individual plant loading. The exclusion of revenue can also maintain confidentiality on sensitive pricing issues. But the uncoupling of revenues from expenses can have serious implications, particularly at the level of the plant. In the absence of revenue as a control factor, the managerial emphasis falls on volume and cost. And 'cost' is used in the specialized sense of 'direct cost' with no recognition of overheads incurred elsewhere on behalf of the plant. Without revenue responsibility, management at plant level can be reduced to 'production management' in its narrowest sense. Production becomes divorced from marketing, the maker from the consumer. Quantity can be esteemed more highly than quality, cost more highly than value. Prospects for revenue enhancement go unseen and improved performance becomes solely a matter of cost reduction.

2. Contribution centre approach

Under the contribution centre approach, a distinction is made between activities which generate revenue (in our example, the thirty plants) and activities which incur expenses without generating material revenue (in our example, HQ, divisions, etc.). The latter are categorized as overhead activities and treated in the same fashion as cost centres in the previous approach. The global revenue of the firm is disaggregated to the revenue-generating activities. Each such activity has identified for it the revenue attributable to a particular period. Against this revenue are charged the expenses directly incurred by that activity. These expenses include no element of the expenses incurred indirectly through the overhead activities.

The result is another specialized form of financial performance. The difference between the sales revenue and the direct expenses of a revenue-generating activity represents not profit or loss but that activity's 'contribution' towards the overhead expenses of running the firm. The revenue-generating activities are 'contribution' centres, the overhead activities 'cost' centres. The P & L Account for the firm in our example would be constructed as follows:

Firm Profit and Loss Account	
£	
Sales Revenue	Separate data for
LESS Direct costs ___	30 plants
Contribution	Data for each cost centre, HQ,
LESS Overheads ___	etc.
Operating profit/loss ___	

The attribution of revenue to plants and similar activities overcomes the major defect of the cost centre approach. Production is re-coupled to sales. But 'cost' at plant level still does not reflect 'full cost'. Overhead is incurred on behalf of all plants and must ultimately be recovered through the contribution from the revenue-generating activities. If overhead is distanced from the plant, 'contribution' can easily be confused with 'operating profit' and financial performance at plant level grossly exaggerated.

3. Profit centre approach

The profit centre approach attempts to resolve both the complexities of disaggregating revenues and the difficulties of including an appropriate share of overheads within the expenses of each individual plant. Revenue is treated in the same way as the contribution centre approach. Overhead expenses continue to be collected on a cost centre basis for the non-revenue-generating activities (HQ, etc.). But the expenses are then apportioned, on an equitable basis, over the revenue-generating activities on whose behalf they have been incurred. As a result the expenses of that activity now contain not only the direct expenses of that activity but also its 'share' of the overhead expenses of the firm. The calculation of the activity's share can be based on many criteria (head-count, space occupied, etc.) but cannot be precise. Precision would involve a prohibitive 'cost of the costing system'. The system of apportioning overheads to revenue-generating activities is usually known as 'full costing'.

The assessment of the individual activity's financial performance now involves three components – revenue, direct expenses, apportioned overhead. It is now possible to construct for the activity, as a measure of financial performance, a P & L Account which replicates in microcosm the P & L Account for the firm. The 'contribution' centre has been transformed into a 'profit' centre:

Plant Profit and Loss Account £	
Sales revenue	Revenue generated locally
LESS Direct costs	Expenses incurred locally
Contribution	Apportionment of total over-head for firm
LESS Overheads	
Operating profit/loss	

The profit centre approach attempts to show the full cost of, in our example, each plant's activities and to match this full cost with revenues generated. Plant management is linked, via the P & L Account, to both the market and the overhead activities of the firm. The financial performance of the plant can be assessed on the same basis as the financial performance of the firm. In terms of measurement, then, there is a fit between plant and firm. However, in terms of accountability, lacunae persist. As we have seen, plant management's responsibility for revenue may be limited while officials at other locations retain responsibility for overhead expenditure. But, even with these imperfections, the profit centre approach does provide plant management with a comprehensive model of the financial workings of the operation under their control. As they say on Barnsley marketplace plant management have been afforded a glimpse of the financial *gestalt*.

It is often argued that the use of full costing can distort the decision-making process. Decisions on plant closure are cited as examples of such distortion. Here, it is argued, reliance should be placed on contribution, not operating profit. Assume that Plant X is making a positive contribution of £3m, in other words, revenues exceed direct expenses by £3m. However, the plant is charged, on an equitable basis, an apportionment of overheads in the sum of £5m. Accordingly, Plant X is incurring an operating loss of £2m. Times are hard, dead wood needs excising, and closure looms. If the loss-maker is eliminated, the financial performance of the firm as a whole will, *ipso facto*, improve. The time has come for Plant X to lay down its life so that the firm may live. But will closure improve overall financial performance?

Assume that the firm's other revenue-generating activities, excluding Plant X, make a total contribution of £100m and absorb overhead expenses of £50m. If closure of Plant X simply means that its share of overheads (£5m) will be re-apportioned over the surviving revenue-generating activities, then closure will lead to a deterioration in financial performance to the extent of Plant X's foregone contribution:

	Firm excl. Plant X	Plant X	Total	Closure of Plant X	Total after Closure
	£m	£m	£m	£m	£m
Contribution	100	3	103	(−) 3	100
Overhead	(50)	(5)	(55)	–	(55)
Operating profit/(loss)	50	(2)	48	(−) 3	45

Hence it is argued that no plant should close so long as it is making a positive financial contribution to the firm's overheads.

The import of the argument must be treated as indicative rather than prescriptive. Decisions on closures and similar issues are not necessarily based on past and present performance but on future expectations. If Plant X's market is short-term, if its plant and equipment are approaching obsolescence, if under-utilized or new capacity elsewhere in the firm can replace Plant X's output at a higher contribution, then the argument from contribution theory is too restrictive. In addition, the 'fixity' of overhead expenditure has increasingly been revealed as mythical. 'Slimdown' operations based on plant closure have often provided the catalyst for decentralization, with a scaling-down of operations at the centre. The number of prestigious former head offices on the property market in central London explode the myth of 'fixed' overheads.

But this is not to reject the usefulness of contribution, simply to ensure that it is used in its proper context. Nor does the use of full costing for purposes of monitoring and control preclude the use of contribution for other purposes.

The profit centre approach, then, aims to replicate the firm's external environment within the firm's individual revenue-generating activities, to confront plant management with the revenue implications of their activities and the full cost of their operations. But, as we have seen, certain activities remain as cost centres. How can a whiff of the market be introduced here to avoid the passive accumulation of expense and its mechanistic apportionment to revenue-generating activities?

Some cost centres lend themselves to treatment as 'internal profit centres'. Such centres do not generate revenue from the external world but an 'internal charge' can be put on the measurable service which they provide to other activities within the firm. In our example, this treatment could be applied to the in-house computer centre. The internal charge may reflect that level of charge which will enable the service activity to recover its costs or to earn an appropriate rate of return on its assets. Any profit made by the activity will be a transaction internal to the firm and will not appear as an addition to profit in the Published Accounts. Where the service provided is less measurable, changes in corporate philosophy can transform cost centres into internal profit centres. For example, some services may be accepted from headquarters uncritically and as a matter of routine: the service is not charged directly but lost in the global overhead apportionment. However, if a direct charge is installed, local management is presented with the bill for its utilization of that service. If the bill is unacceptable, then utilization must be reduced or alternatives, inside and outside the firm, adopted. The heady brew of competition bubbles through the firm. Services like Training and Internal Consultancy have to sell their wares within the firm and ensure that price and quality are competitive with the external alternatives.

Some cost centres, then, are susceptible to the 'profit centre' approach. The user of the service sees the cost clearly in his P & L Account: utilization of the service can be monitored and controlled at local level. The provider of the service is sensitive to the price and quality of the bought-in alternative: price and quality can be monitored and controlled. In brief, the extension of profit centre thinking to cost centres puts financial values on internal services, compares these values with similar services available externally and brings market pressures to bear on parts of the firm traditionally immune to such forces.

So far, in discussing the profit centre approach, we have not gone beyond the level of 'operating profit'. Interest on borrowings has not been allocated to profit centres. As such, the profit centre does not replicate the firm as a whole. Interest represents a cost, the cost of financing the profit centre's fixed and current assets. If it is absent from the profit centre's P & L Account the full costs of the profit centre are not being revealed. There can be technical difficulties in assigning interest to individual profit centres: if the firm has a central marketing organization, stocks of product may be determined in the best interests of the firm rather than of individual plants. But without interest we do not see full cost. If interest is introduced at local level, we are moving from the profit centre to the investment centre approach, with the revenue-generating activity able to monitor and control not only its full P & L Account but also its balance sheet and cash flow. The revenue-generating activities, either individually or in appropriate groupings, take on the persona of stand alone companies. The firm has become a collection of separate business units.

Effective management of the P & L Account demands the imposition of measurability and accountability upon diverse financial phenomena. In pursuit of such commodities we have identified three key variables – revenues, direct costs and overhead expenses. We have seen that these variables can be arranged into cost, contribution or profit centres. Let us assume that the profit centre approach is adopted. An effective management system will need to monitor and control three types of financial activity:

(a) *Cost centres:* activities which incur costs but do not generate material revenue: the function performed is not suited to a system of internal charging based on discrete services supplied to other activities within the firm, i.e. HQ, Finance Department, Chief Executive's Office etc. where the cost is incurred for the firm as a whole.

(b) *Cost/internal service centres:* activities which do provide discrete services for which charge can be rendered to individual activities on the basis of utilization i.e. central computer facilities, internal road transport services, central training establishments etc.

(c) *Profit centres:* activities which generate substantial external revenue and incur costs.

A share of Activity (a) costs will be apportioned to profit centres. Activity (b) costs will be charged to profit centres on the basis of utilization. All costs, then, will eventually come to be borne by the profit centres. The process of financial monitoring and control at this level needs to be examined in detail.

Assume that the plant has four production lines. Each 'track' generates revenue and incurs 'prime' cost – wages of operatives, materials and power consumed and other items directly related to the production process. In addition, 'internal' overheads are incurred in two forms:

(a) production overhead: production services like maintenance, storekeeping, etc. are provided in common for all production lines;

(b) non-operational overhead: managerial and administrative services are provided at the plant for the plant as a whole.

The prime costs, production overhead and non-operational overhead, are all incurred at local level. In addition, as we have seen, 'external' overhead will be charged to the plant as a profit centre. Where this overhead comprises a measurable service, the charge will be based on utilization. Otherwise a global sum will simply be apportioned in respect of services remotely rendered.

So, effective management of the P & L Account will need to cover the following items:

(a) revenue generated, in the example, by four production lines;
(b) prime costs: wages, materials etc. directly attributable to each of the production lines;
(c) internal overhead: (i) production overhead – maintenance, storekeeping, etc.;
(ii) non-operational overhead – management, administration, etc.;
(d) external overhead: (i) services charged on utilization;
(ii) global apportionment on lump-sum basis.

Before any system of monitoring and control can be established at the plant, the relevant items, appropriately disaggregated, must be available in measurable form. Responsibility can then be assigned to individuals for the financial management of items or part-items and the individuals can be held accountable on a regular basis for performance against a budgetted standard. In our example, the four production lines can stand as 'contribution centres' (direct revenue less prime costs). Internal overhead can be disaggregated to functional departments on a cost centre basis and the relevant functional heads held responsible and accountable. The 'services' element of external overhead can be similarly assigned to a responsible official. Apportioned external overhead may appear to be a 'given', beyond the control of plant management. However the political process of the firm may enable pressure to be applied on the windpipe of remote cost centres. Lower the cost or we either buy-in the service from outside or perform it in-house at plant level.

The prime instrument for monitoring and control in such a system will be a statement of financial performance (cost or contribution) in a particular period compared with budget, how we *have* performed compared with how we *ought* to have performed. So, the responsible officials in the system will receive the relevant statement and can be held accountable for the variances between actual and budgetted financial performance. But two problems need to be overcome before the system can approach effectiveness.

First, the system as described only provides monitoring and control after the event – *ex post facto* as the denizens of Barnsley would say. Now there is a school of management thought which holds that we learn our most powerful lessons from our mistakes; ignore the mistakes of the past and we repeat them in the present; history repeats itself etc., etc. Unfortunately, while this powerful learning experience is taking place, in terms of the corporate coffers the cash is over the hill and far away. Control must be exercised at source. Two questions are relevant:

(i) within a cost or contribution centre, who authorizes what expenditure?
(ii) against what standard is the authorization given?

Answers to the first question might reveal that high-cost items require detailed authorization. However, the bulk of expenditure comprises low-value, high-volume items and for these authorization is a matter of routine. Answers to the second question might reveal that authorizations are given against production schedules which do not reconcile with the financial budget.

The second problem to be overcome relates to the precise nature of the responsibility assigned to individuals for cost and contribution centres. A simplistic system would assign responsibility for revenue and prime costs to 'line' managers, responsibility for internal and external overheads to functional heads of department. But consider in detail the financial statement for one of the four production lines: assume that all production in the relevant period has been sold. Revenue is a function of the number of units produced and the price realized per unit. The latter may well be outside the line manager's control, a responsibility of the marketing department. Again, if prime costs are examined, the utilization of direct labour and material may be a responsibility of line management but wage rates and materials' prices may be negotiated by functional departments. Similarly, if financial statements for cost centres are examined, responsibilities are not necessarily self-contained. Personnel costs may be high as a result of high labour turnover: the solution may well lie not with the personnel specialist but with the line manager. Most items of revenue cost will contain both a 'line' and a 'functional' element. Figure 13 depicts this phenomenon.

If the accountability process treats the 'line' and the 'functions' in isolation, micro-politics can take over. The 'line' will attempt to shift the boundary of responsibility downwards and to the left, the 'functions' upward and to the right. The responsibility system becomes irresponsible. An effective system needs to integrate 'line' and 'functional' responsibilities.

Systems, then, need to be devised to make sense of diverse financial phenomena and to enable individuals to monitor, control and be held accountable for financial performance. The basis of

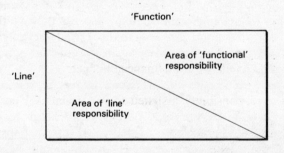

Figure 13: *Allocation of responsibility*

this accountability will be performance against a budgetted standard. Before the construction of such standards can be examined, another factor must be considered: the way in which differnt costs within the system behave.

Behaviour may seem a strange concept to apply to inanimate objects like costs. However, different costs do behave differently when the level of production changes. A sensitivity to these behavioural patterns is essential if financial performance is to be understood and sensible budgets compiled for the future.

Let us return to the plant in the example. Some costs bear a direct relationship to the level of production: if production rises, they rise proportionally: if production falls, so do they. Raw material input to a manufacturing process, with standard consumption per unit of production, provides a good example; similarly, wages under a piecework system. Costs which bear such a direct relationship to changes in the level of production are known as variable costs.

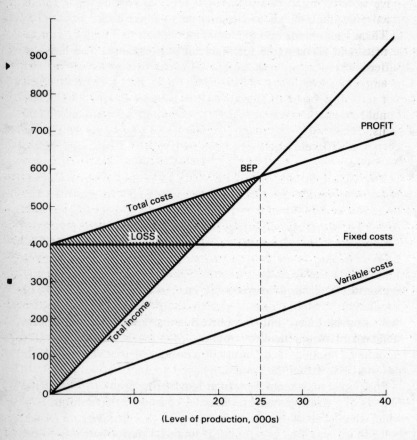

Figure 14: *Cost/volume/profit model*

Other costs do not have such a relationship to changes in level of production. They remain unaffected by such changes. Examples are depreciation, factory rental, day-wage systems of payment, etc. These costs are known as fixed costs.

Finally, there are costs which contain elements of both the variable and fixed behaviour patterns. So, electricity charges may reflect a fixed standing charge plus an amount per unit consumed.

These items are known as semi-variable costs. Variable costs have a direct relationship with the level of production whereas fixed costs tend to be a function of time.

These insights into the behaviour of costs enable models to be constructed for revenues and costs, both fixed and variable, at different volumes of production. Assume that the plant in our example has fixed costs of £400k p.a. Variable costs amount to £8 per unit of production. Production is sold at £24 per unit. The annual production capacity of the plant is assessed at 40,000 units. Financial performance (revenue (−) [variable (+) fixed costs]) at different volumes of production is illustrated at Figure 14.

Fixed costs do not vary with changes in the level of output. Items like rental and depreciation are the same whether the level is 0 or 40,000 units p.a. Accordingly, the fixed cost line is parallel to the horizontal axis. Variable costs rise proportionally with production at the rate of £8 per unit of production. The total cost line is derived by superimposing the variable cost function on the fixed cost function. Income rises proportionally with the level of production at the rate of £24 per unit of production. Total income intersects the total cost line at 25,000 units of production. This is the break-even point (BEP). BEP can be checked arithmetically:

$$\text{BEP} = \frac{\text{total fixed costs}}{\text{sales income per unit } (-) \text{ variable cost per unit}}$$

$$\text{BEP} = \frac{400,000}{16} = 25,000 \text{ units}$$

At the point of intersection, the angle of the total income line is greater than the angle of the total cost line. Beyond the break-even point, fixed costs, by definition, stay the same. Total profit is increased by the marginal contribution (£16) of each additional unit production.

Hence:

Level of Production Units (k)	Contribution £k	Fixed Costs £k	Profit £k
25,000	400	400	b/even
30,000	480	400	80
35,000	560	400	160
40,000	640	400	240

Between 30 and 40,000 units, a 33 per cent increase in production has caused profits to increase by a factor of three. If the incidence of fixed costs ('operational gearing or leverage') is high, relatively small changes in the level of production can cause significant shifts in financial performance.

Again, the results of break-even analysis should be treated as indicative rather than prescriptive. Broad assumptions have to be made in assessing the variability and fixity of many items of costs. Assumptions are also made about the ability of the market to absorb output without dilution of revenue. Also, there must be capacity limitations. As these limitations are approached, cost relationships may alter as overtime is worked and maintenance costs escalate. Extension of capacity may involve additional machines, with a 'step' increase in the fixed cost function. However, the model does draw out the relationship of the volume of production to profitability in a cost structure with a high incidence of fixed costs.

So, the firm has organized itself, through a series of cost, contribution and profit centres, to manage the P & L Account. Measurability is achieved and individuals are held to account either for costs or for contribution (revenues and direct costs), or for profit (revenues and full costs) in a system of 'responsibility accounting'. The importance of controlling expenditure at source and of managing the boundary between 'line' and 'functional' reponsibilities has been grasped. Finally the firm has a model, albeit approximate, of the cost/volume/profit relationships within its various activities.

The standard by which actual performance is monitored and controlled is the budget. Much has been written on the motivational aspects of budgetting. Should the budget be descriptive, and simply project into the future current performance adjusted for known changes? Or should the budget go further and implant improvement factors over and above past experience and known future changes? Should it explicitly contain an element of targetry, attempt to stretch managers and seek, from ordinary people, extraordinary performance? Or is such hyperbole counterproductive? Have managers outsmarted motivational theory and become cynical about carrots, world-weary about sticks?

In most cases, discussions about whether budgets should be normative or descriptive are interesting but not particularly useful. When you're up to the butt in alligators, you don't worry about draining the swamp. The simple reality of business, particularly in the era of recession, is that the firm, unless seduced into soft objectives, *needs* improved performance from many of its constituent parts.

When the firm, as part of the objective-setting process, considers potential performance in the future, it has as its base the *fait accompli* of current performance and past experience. Within current performance there may be changes – organizational, attitudinal, investment-led – which have not yet fructified. In addition, further changes may be planned or anticipated in the near future. In other words, if we project the current reality into the future, adjust for the full burgeoning of past change and the impact of future change, we have, *ipso facto*, improved performance. But is such improvement sufficient? Or is there a gap between where we are headed and where we want to be? Figure 15 summarizes the position of shortfall.

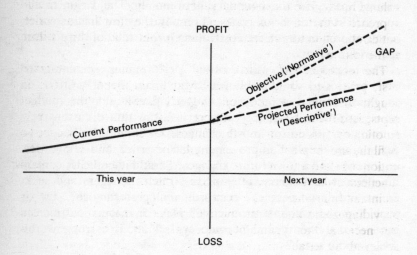

Figure 15: *The budgetary gap*

We have a gap between 'what ought to be' and 'what, on best information, is likely to be'. If the firm believes that the gap will be bridged by some magic of synergy or an inexorable progression along an experience curve, it is not merely believing in miracles, it is positively relying on them. Corporate Couéism – 'every day in every way we are getting a little bit better' – is not enough. The gap needs to be analyzed and plans laid for its bridging.

In seeking improved financial performance, the cost/profit/ volume model provides a useful tool for considering alternatives. The model contains the main determinants of financial per- formance – volume of production (if sold), selling price per unit, variable cost per unit and fixed costs. Obviously an improvement in one or a combination of these determinants provides the means for bridging the performance gap.

Cost reduction will usually form one of the components in a performance improvement policy, particularly when markets are tight. At plant level, variable costs provide a tempting target. In a high-volume process where plant is operating at full capacity, the merest sliver off variable cost per unit can translate, if price and volume holds, into a substantial sum of money. The danger in this approach is that it concentrates on cost and, by implication, price but can be blind to a third factor, namely the value of the product to the customer.

The technique of 'value analysis' (VA) attempts to integrate cost, price and value when improved financial performance is sought through cost reduction. 'Value', like most abstract concepts, is difficult to define with precision. Within the concept is a notion of 'functionalism' – the ability of the product or service to fulfil the use for which it was acquired. The concept also contains a notion of 'attractiveness' – characteristics beyond the purely functional which encourage purchase. The objective of VA is to maintain full value to the customer while reducing the cost of providing such value. It is concerned with the elimination of costs not necessary to the maintenance of value. This can only be achieved by establishing a closeness to cost and, above all, a closeness to the customer. VA is, therefore, a multi-disciplinary technique which crashes departmental frontiers and broadens perspectives beyond the plant and its products to the customers and his preferences. As such, it can provide a framework for integrating production, provisioning, finance and marketing.

The practice is straightforward. Each product is systematically examined by a multi-disciplinary team. The product is disaggregated into its constituent parts. The direct cost of each component part in terms of bought-in price, cost of manufacturing time, etc., is analyzed. The value of the component part, 'functional' and 'attractive', to the consumer is similarly assessed. In all that follows, the maintenance of this value to the customer is the limiting factor. The aim is to reduce cost without diminishing value. A range of questions is triggered:

Does the constituent part add value or can it, like the second striking surface on a matchbox, be discarded without loss of value?

If the constituent part is bought-in, can it be acquired more cheaply from another supplier?

Can another component, another material, a different technology, deliver the same value at lower cost?

The result may be innovatory – new processes, new materials; or creative – new relationships fashioned from existing variables. Whether innovatory or creative, the proposal is validated with the customer before change is implemented. VA is usually associated with variable costs where the constituents, although of low value, have high utilization. The cost saving per unit of production may appear insignificant but, when multiplied by the total volume of production, produces a substantial saving. With value maintained, price and sales volume unchanged, this cost saving will flow through to the bottom line of the P & L Account as pure gain to operating profit.

There is another spin-off from techniques like VA. We have examined the content of VA. The 'process' of the technique offers a wide range of opportunities for the development and improvement of managerial knowledge, skills and competences. Burgoyne, Boydell and Pedler identify eleven qualities which, research suggests, more effective managers possess in greater abundance than their less effective confrères:

   (i) command of basic facts about the firm's products, markets, people etc.

  (ii) relevant professional knowledge

 (iii) sensitivity to events, the ability to perceive movements in the firm's environment

 (iv) analytical, problem-solving and decision/judgement-making skills

  (v) social skills and abilities, including the ability to resolve conflict, persuade, use and respond to power

 (vi) emotional resilience, the ability to cope with stress

 (vii) proactivity, the ability to take initiatives

(viii) creativity

 (ix) mental agility

  (x) balanced learning habits and skills, the capability of both abstract and concrete thought

 (xi) self-knowledge

The multi-disciplinary, team-based approach of VA provides opportunities for insights into most of the above qualities. As such, the technique can be a rich source of managerial learning.

The concept of value can also offer glimpses of the quirkiness of consumers and their preferences. Around the time that our friend Baron Edmund de Rothschild was nibbling at his grapes, Marcus Samuel was setting up Shell. The major product, in the pre-automotive age, was kerosene. An important market was Indonesia, supplied from the oilfields in Burma. In those days, the product was sold in tin cans mainly as a fuel for cooking and light. Then came the invention of the petrol pump. Ahead of the competition, Samuel saw the impact this development could have on distributional costs. Use value remained the same. The switch was made and sales . . . plummeted. Quite simply, the value of the product to the customer extended beyond use value. There was also a notion of attractiveness. The attractiveness lay not in the kerosene but in its container, the tin can. Beaten, it could be used as a roofing material; forged it became a plough; untouched it served as a receptacle for diverse fluids, as a cooking pot, a bath; perforated, it was a brazier. The poetry lay not in the product but in the packaging.

VA, then, tends to focus on variable costs. But, these days, the problem for monitoring and control systems is not so much the variable as the fixed costs of the firm. Variable costs have an objective reference point in the volume of production. There is symmetry between changes in such volume and changes in the level of variable costs incurred. At any level of output, the firm knows what variable costs 'ought' to be.

But when we move from variable to fixed costs, the reference point of the level of production is no longer valid. By definition, fixed costs are not a function of production levels. Nor is there an alternative reference point to indicate, with objectivity, what the level of fixed costs 'ought' to be. What, for example, is the 'objective' level of expenditure for advertising, management development, R & D? With no objective reference point, control becomes difficult. But the need for control becomes increasingly pertinent as the proportion of fixed costs in corporate cost-structures continues to rise inexorably. Many factors have contributed to this rise.

Labour costs have, to a large extent, been transformed from a variable into a fixed cost. Payment systems have moved from being largely determined by output (the 'piece'), with a small daywage element, to being largely determined by time, with a small 'bonus' element. Labour 'oncosts' have increased substantially: holiday pay, sick pay, pension contributions, even private health subscriptions, are totally unrelated to the level of output. Capital intensity has increased both in office and factory: depreciation, a fixed cost, comprises a larger and larger item in cost structures. Organizations have expanded in size and complexity in the quest for economies of scale. The quest has led to centralization, with central functions growing faster than the operating areas. Technology has facilitated such centralization. Organizational size and complexity have increased the number of purely co-ordinating functions. Social attitudes, the 'revolution of rising expectations' and the 'assertive society', have all had an impact on the cost-structure of the firm. The environmental revolution and principles like 'the polluter pays' have substantially added to costs, from rows of trees and beds of flowers to sophisticated emission-control devices. Society now demands clean air, water and earth as well as cheap products and jobs. The effective management of the financial territory needs effective monitoring and control of fixed costs.

The traditional approach to determining an appropriate level of fixed costs for next year is to use the current year as the base. Typically, an overhead department or other cost centre is treated as a global sum of money rather than as a series of separately costed activities. Using the current year as a base, a uniform percentage increase or decrease is laid down for next year. The use of a uniform change factor for all cost centres implies that all are equally effective and efficient. The system also places great importance on the current year's expenditure. If this year is known to be the base for next year's allocation, the name of the game is never, ever to underspend and diminish the base. Increasingly desperate attempts to avoid the sin of underspending are usually concentrated on the period immediately before the year-end. The result is known as the 'hockey-stick effect' (Figure. 16).

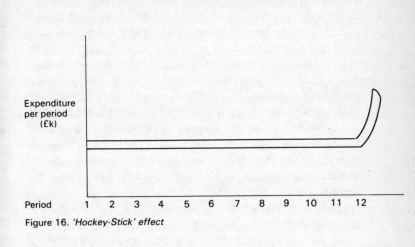

Figure 16. *'Hockey-Stick' effect*

Figure 16: *'Hockey-Stick' effect*

The cost centre consumes resources at an even rate in the first eleven accounting periods of the year. Resource consumption is below budgetted levels. It realizes, to its horror, that if such moderation is allowed to continue, it will underspend on budget and the underspend will reduce the base from which next year's budget is determined. Accordingly, moderation is branded as meanness of spirit and a crash programme of expenditure is undertaken in Period 12 to take up this year's allocation and maintain intact the base for next year.

The uncritical use of expenditure in the current year as the determinant of control data in the future is obviously a seriously flawed method of establishing appropriate levels of expenditure in the area of fixed costs. The rise of fixed costs becomes 'index-linked'. But traditional methods of severing such linkages also have their limitations. Some of these methods are considered below:

(i) Across the board cuts: the same percentage reduction in expenditure is applied to each cost centre. This seems 'fair' and all become comrades in the same adversity. However, uniformity of treatment can easily be confused with equality of treatment. In applying across the board cuts, each cost centre is treated as a global sum of money, not as a set of activities which may or may not be dispensable. The efficient department is treated on a par with the inefficient department. The cost centre which should be growing withers while the centre which should be declining continues to bloom. But if special cases are introduced and dispensations issued to deserving cases, the firm soon discovers that the easiest way to make enemies is to do someone a favour. And while friends come and go, enemies simply accumulate;

(ii) appeals to moderation and parsimony or the 'brush your teeth in the dark' approach: 'Times are hard, work off some fat, tighten your belts and pull up the drawbridge.' Such management by exhortation is likely to leave carnivorous heads of spending departments quite unmoved. The approach is not unlike an appeal to a tiger to consider the merits of vegetarianism;

(iii) 'Let's partition Poland again': faced with pressure for reductions, the mighty form an alliance and leave the meek exposed. Such 'extravagant' or 'discretionary' items as tra ning, research and development, advertising etc. are squeezed until the pips squeak. Another slice is taken off the salami of corporate 'profligacy' while, in the more powerful cost centres, life continues on its even tenor;

(iv) detailed departmental investigations or 'paralysis by analysis': such investigations, whether conducted in-house or by external consultants, are both expensive and time-consuming. If commissioned to focus on one specific cost centre, linkages with other centres may be overlooked. If commissioned as a short-term response to burgeoning fixed costs, the process may smack of 'management by crisis'.

In the absence of an objective reference point, the firm has to decide what, in total, it can afford in the form of fixed costs. Having decided its total expenditure, the firm is then confronted with the classical political situation of infinite demands on these finite resources. In firms where power is concentrated in few people or in an ideology, allocation of these finite resources may be based on inadequate knowledge of the detailed activities for which global sums of money are being assigned on a cost centre or departmental basis. In firms where power is more widely diffused, a similar lack of information on which to discuss alternatives can reduce the process of allocation to the level of the pork-barrel. Defence of the cost centre's budget can become the ultimate virility symbol. Information is crucial to an effective system of allocation. Traditional methods of budgetting in the area of fixed costs do not provide such information in relevant form. But attempts to isolate such information through detailed investigation can result in 'analysis paralysis'.

Zero Base Budgetting (ZBB) offers a theory and techniques for the improvement of budgetting and control in the area of fixed overhead costs. The theory is commonsensical:

   (i) in formulating budgets in this area, do not be distracted by past or current expenditure

  (ii) focus not on sums of money but on the specific activities which comprise the overhead territory

 (iii) start from a base of zero and contemplate all these activities anew

 (iv) substantiate proposals for continuation of activities without reference to what was done in the past

  (v) 'ignore the past and start from scratch'

Within this theoretical framework, a detailed approach has been developed, initially by Peter Pyhrr. The approach starts with a process of disaggregation. Global cost centres are broken down into the smallest, indivisible 'activity units'. An activity unit is the smallest constituent of the cost centre which, in terms of activities and objectives, can be free-standing. So, the global cost centre 'personnel' will be disaggregated into myriad activity units like recruitment, rates of pay, training, pensions, etc.

Having isolated the activity units, the approach next identifies the ways in which the unit carries out its work. These procedures are examined and alternatives sought. For example, the activity unit 'training' may operate by running courses in-house at one central location. Alternative procedures might involve a decentralization of such courses to in-house *local* centres or the appointment of an external agent to mount the courses at locations outside the firm. The costs and benefits of each procedure are calculated and compared with the current procedure. Within each activity unit, a range of alternatives has been generated and quantified.

'Levels of effort' are then introduced. A 'minimum' level of effort is determined below which the activity unit could produce no worthwhile outputs. In our example, this might comprise the minimum number of trainers and trainees required for the training activity to retain a useful function in the firm. An 'incremental' level of effort is also postulated: this represents the activity unit's view on what it could achieve if additional funds were available. These levels of effort are duly evaluated and compared with the current level of effort. Whereas, under traditional methods, the costs of the activity unit were lost in a global departmental total, they are now isolated. Whereas procedures and levels of effort risked being accepted as 'givens', a series of alternatives has now been generated. Analysis has replaced simple description.

Having generated a constellation of alternative procedures and levels of effort, the activity unit now makes its choice. It constructs a 'decision-package' which shows both its preferences and the alternatives discarded. The package represents an incremental ranking of preferred alternatives: if only £50k were available to the activity unit, the unit would be forced to operate at the minimum level of effort with that level's concomitant procedures. If an additional £30k were available, the unit could maintain its current level of effort and its current procedures. If a further £20k were available, at this incremental level of effort, new procedures could be implemented with a benefit of £X to the firm. The decision-packages of the activity units are re-aggregated into a decision-package for the cost centre as a whole. All the alternatives are ranked and an appropriate financial cut-off point applied at that level of expenditure which the firm can afford. The process continues in an upward direction through the firm.

The approach has distinct advantages. Global totals are avoided and an analysis of activities is undertaken. The process of contributing to the budget is decentralized to the level of individual activity units. Alternatives are generated and evaluated. Choice is introduced to the process. Detailed analysis can be a powerful source of organizational learning and there is always a store of alternatives, just below the cut-off point, which can be implemented if funds become available.

The analysis also informs the political process. Specific activities, ideas and alternatives are now the stuff of the political process rather than global sums of money. The cost of rejected alternatives is available and the opportunity cost of a particular preference can be assessed.

Value analysis and zero base budgetting can be too easily dismissed as 'what we have been doing, *de facto* if not *de jure*, for years'. But is this quite the case? Like most good ideas, both VA and ZBB are applied commonsense. But is commonsense applied in the firm on a systematic basis and focussed in detail on individual products and cost centres? Does what is commonsensical for the customer necessarily infuse the design and manufacture of the product? Are alternative procedures and differing levels of effort taken into account in evaluating cost centres? To dismiss the techniques as 'old hat' is to miss the point. In management, as in most human activities, there are few new ideas: simply old ideas given new currency.

The effective management of that region of the financial territory which is dominated by the P & L Account requires an appropriate organizational structure wherein sense is made of diverse financial phenomena. The various approaches – cost, contribution and profit centres – have been considered. Within the structure, costs will behave in different ways as the level of production changes. In seeking financial improvement in the future, the importance of 'gap analysis' has been noted. Value analysis has been discussed as an approach to improvement in the variable cost area. Zero base budgetting has been similarly discussed with reference to the area of fixed costs.

From all this, it should be apparent that the figures in the P & L Account, though expressed in a specialized language, do not exist in isolation. The figures simply reflect the activities, attitudes and preferences of those employed in the real physical world of products and services, men and machines, suppliers and customers. In this sense the bottom line, profit or loss, is not a cause, it is an effect.

6. Managing Working Capital and the Capital Structure

1. Working capital

As we have seen, the term 'working capital' refers to a firm's net investment in short-term assets:

	£
Stocks	x
Debtors	x
Cash and bank	x
Current assets	x
LESS Current liabilities	(x)
Working capital (net current assets)	x

The concept of working capital (or 'circulating capital') has pre-industrial origins. In the days when most 'manufacturies' were adjuncts of agriculture, processors would buy in produce immediately after the harvest. Cash would flow out of the processors' coffers. The raw material acquired would be duly processed and put to stock. At this stage in the cycle there would be a heavy demand for working capital to finance the stocks. Pharaoh may have been far-sighted in stocking his granaries during the seven years of plenty but that corn was eating its head off in interest payments. Finance usually came in the form of short-term loans. But the stocks would gradually be sold and cash would flow back into the firm. Stocks would be cleared before the next harvest, the loans would be repaid and the cycle would begin again. Working capital circulated through the firm and completed its cycle, with a seasonal symmetry, by finding its way back to its providers. Fixed asset replacement or expansion was a separate matter to be financed by retained profits or external long-term funds. Herein lies the classical notion that working capital should be financed short-term and fixed assets long-term.

But as the rural gave way to the urban, as industry moved away from its agricultural base and as agriculture turned itself into 'agribusiness', production and financial cycles became less dominated by the symmetry of the seasons. And as the scale and complexity of industry increased, it became apparent that working capital in total was not necessarily self-liquidating. A high-volume manufacturing concern would maintain a buffer stock of raw materials and bought-in components as insurance against uncertainties in supply. A similar stock of finished product would be retained to guard against production shortfalls or distributional problems. Goods would be sold and services supplied not for cash but on credit terms. Accordingly, an amount of money would always be outstanding to the firm from debtors.

In this context, working capital came to be divided into two tranches. One tranche represented the 'permanent working capital' of the firm and was, in effect, as firmly sunk in the firm as a long-lived fixed asset. The other tranche did 'circulate', in the pre-industrial sense, as a function of seasonality, abnormalities of supply and production, and other factors. The notion of 'permanent working capital' called into question the classical assumption that working capital should be financed short-term. 'Permanent assets' imply long-term funding.

The notion of permanent working capital is particularly important when sales are growing and/or capital expenditure of an expansionary nature is planned. In the euphoria of increased sales, it is easy to overlook the concomitant implications for working capital. If the volume of sales increases, greater funds may be required to finance a permanent increase in debtors and stocks (raw materials, work in progress and finished goods). To the extent that these increases cannot be offset by improved terms from creditors, additional funds will be required on a permanent basis.

If such funds are not secured, the firm can find itself in a position of 'overtrading'. Assume that the increased sales are made on sixty days' credit. Raw materials are purchased on thirty days' credit. The conversion process takes five days. Obviously, there is a gap between the creditor's settlement day and the date when the debtor pays up. The product may be excellent, the process highly efficient, the sales prospects rosy, but unless additional funding is secured, managerial endeavour can easily be diverted from maintaining the expansionary impetus to keeping the creditor wolf from the corporate door.

Effective management in the area of working capital must concern itself with determining the 'optimum' level of stock, debtors, etc., to be maintained. Current assets will vary with sales but the required ratio of current assets to sales is a policy matter. If the firm elects to operate aggressively it will hold minimum levels of stock, allow limited credit periods to customers and demand long lines of credit from suppliers. The funding requirement will be reduced and the rate of return on capital employed will increase. The real, however, is often but a shadow of the ideal, particularly if you are a small company drawing supplies from, and selling products to, Leviathans. In these situations the small company learns that 'he has the power who needs the other less'. For the small company to persuade its Big Brothers to settle promptly for purchases and, at the same time, give long credit on supplies is about as easy as pushing a pound of melting butter into a tiger's ear-hole with a red-hot pin. In addition, aggression carries with it considerable risks. Low stock levels, of raw materials or finished product, increase the probability of stock-outs; tight credit terms diminish the marketing appeal of the product; long credit lines may produce an overdependence on a single source of supply. Determination of the 'optimum' policy for items of working capital involves a complex balancing of risk against return.

But the control of working capital is not simply a numbers game. Working capital reductions are not secured by arithmetic, however complex, but by physical actions in the real world of the firm. For many manufacturing concerns, stocks of raw materials, bought-in components and assemblies comprise a major component of working capital. In Japan in the early 1970s, Toyota was acutely conscious of this fact. Such stockholdings were not only expensive in terms of working capital, they also required stock-points and warehousing facilities. Valuable space was being occupied and the multiple handling involved added to costs without contributing to value. So why, Toyota asked itself, were stockholdings maintained at such levels? First, the stocks were held as a buffer against the supplier's inability to deliver in the right quantity at the right time. Secondly, the stocks were held in such quantities to provide time to inspect for quality defects. If the 'buffer' element of stocks was to be eliminated, co-ordinated action was required with the suppliers. Thus was born the 'kanban' or 'just in time' system of stock control. Suppliers' production systems and schedules were redesigned to synchronize exactly with Toyota's assembly systems and schedules: the supplier delivered, at specified times, direct from the end of his production track to the appropriate point of use in Toyota's assembly line. And quality control systems, physical and human, were installed in the suppliers' plants, to Toyota's specification, to produce 'zero defects'. As a result, buffer stocks were eliminated, working capital reduced, space released for assembly expansion, and multiple handling terminated. Value was maintained and cost much reduced.

Monitoring and control systems for working capital usually involve a series of ratios. Actual ratios can be compared with budget or with performance in competitor firms. The major ratios are:

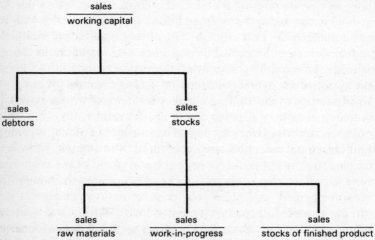

(NOTE: The divisor is usually calculated as the average of levels at start and end of period.)

The overriding ratio, sales/working capital, indicates the number of times the firm should (budget) or does (actual) 'turn over' its working capital in a specified period. The higher the turnover, the greater the velocity at which cash circulates within the firm and the lower the working capital requirement.

That spectacularly successful multinational corporation, Cosa Nostra, soon recognized the importance of cash velocity to business expansion. Joe Valachi, recusant member of the Genovese family, grasped the point when he began to diversify his business operations from the entertainment and leisure sector into personal financial services:

> Now I take some of my profits from the numbers (game) and go into shylocking. The loans went for 20% interest, which is what we call vigorish. Take an example. You loan out $1000 and the guy is supposed to pay back $100 per week for twelve weeks. The $200 you make is the vigorish. Figure it another way. For every $5 you lend out a week, you get back $6 . . . Naturally, as soon as the money comes in, I would give it to somebody else. It circulates. By the time it circulates around, I never could figure out what the percentage is I'm getting on it. You would need an accountant to figure that out.

So if in our firm annual sales are £80m and average working capital is £16m, the firm turns over its working capital five times. If this figure is out of line with budgetted working capital turnover or with that achieved by competitor firms, the various contributory ratios (sales/debtors and sales/stocks) can be investigated.

The sales/debtors ratio is usually known as 'debtor turnover'. With annual sales of £80m and average debtors of, say, £8m, the debtor turnover is ten. This turnover can be translated into the number of days' sales tied up in debtors by applying the formula:

$$\frac{365}{\text{debtor turnover}}$$

In our example, the number of days' sales outstanding is 36½. In other words, customers take an average of 36½ days before settling. If the firm's official credit terms are less than this period, there is some weakness in the credit control system or special deals are being struck. If the average credit period could be reduced to thirty-three days, debtor turnover would grow to over eleven and the velocity at which cash circulated in the business would be increased. In cases where companies sell both for cash and on credit, only credit sales should be used in calculating debtor turnover.

The sales/stocks ratio is usually known as 'stock turnover'. The ratio indicates how quickly stock in total and in each of its component parts (raw materials, work-in-progress and finished product) is moving through and out of the business. In financial terms quicker (a high stock turnover) usually means better, but a high stock turnover may be the precursor to stock-outs. Movements in the overall sales/working capital ratio can often be traced to the various stock ratios. Modern capital-intensive, continuous process industries often have all the manoeuvreability of a supertanker. Sales can drop faster than the manufacturer's ability to cut back on production. In this situation, sales revenue declines but stocks build up and the sales/stock ratio is squeezed from both ends. In 1984, sales of home computers soared in the UK. Total sales reached £350m. The market seemed set for further growth. By mid-1985, market estimates were being frantically reduced. Total sales for 1985 were estimated at less than £250m. As a result, sales were dropping, stocks were rising and firms like Sinclair Research were caught in the squeeze of the nutcracker.

Two caveats need to be entered about stock ratios. First, conventional procedure is to calculate stocks as the average of opening and closing figures shown in the balance sheet. This may disguise seasonal fluctuations. For example, 65 per cent of home computers are sold in the UK in the last three months of the year. Secondly 'cost of sales' should be used rather than 'sales'. 'Cost of sales', as we have seen, excludes the profit margin included in 'sales' and, as such, is more appropriate when compared with stocks valued at cost. 'Cost of sales' is available from the internal management accounts of the firm but need not be disclosed in published accounts.

Stock turnover is particularly important in the retail sector. Comparisons can be illuminating. From published accounts (using sales rather than cost of sales) a sample of High Street retailers had the following stock turnovers in 1982:

	Stock Turnover (1982)
	(no. of times)
Currys	7.2
W. H. Smith	10.2
Sainsbury's	14.8

Why the diversity? Obviously the nature of the merchandise retailed is important. Consumer durables (Currys) move more slowly than books, magazines, newspapers, records and stationery (W. H. Smith). In turn, food (Sainsbury's) moves fastest of all. Comparison becomes more meaningful when contrasts are drawn between firms in the same sector of the market. Compare Sainsbury's stock turnover with that of its competitors:

	Stock Turnover (1982)
Sainsbury's	14.8
ASDA	15.5
Wm. Morrison	13.4
Tesco	10.8

Again, mix of merchandise can account for some of the differences. Diversification away from groceries may reduce the ratio. But can all of the differences be so explained? 'Retail is detail.' Is there some detail, some technique which we are ignoring and our competitors are not? Comparative data of this nature can trigger off a series of discriminating questions. The use of ratios is further explored in Chapter 9.

2. Capital structure

The 'capital employed' section of the balance sheet (Chapter 3) contains the capital structure of the firm. This structure usually comprises two components:

(i) shareholders' funds (equity)
(ii) long-term liabilities (debt)

Equity represents the permanent capital of the firm although there is now, in the UK, limited provision under the Companies Act for a firm to buy back its ordinary shares. In the US, buy-backs are both legal and widespread. Debt constitutes the semi-permanent capital of the firm. When a particular loan matures, the firm may reduce its total indebtedness by repaying the debt from retained earnings, realized assets or a new issue of shares. Alternatively, the maturing loan may simply be replaced by a new loan and indebtedness maintained at the same level. Equity and debt are examined, in turn, below.

In the balance sheet, shareholders' funds (equity) is made up of two items:

(i) issued share capital
(ii) reserves

An issue of shares brings cash into the firm. The amount of cash harvested represents the number of shares issued multiplied by the issue price per share less issuing expenses. The scale of these expenses has been revealed by recent privatization issues. Typically, the shares will carry a nominal or 'par value' but will be issued at a premium.

For balance sheet purposes, the cash brought into the firm by an issue of shares is divided into two categories:

(i) the amount realized by the nominal value of the shares;
(ii) the amount attributable to the premium realized.

The latter amount is reduced by the issuing expenses.

So if a firm, on commencement, issued ten thousand ordinary shares with a nominal value of £1 per share at an issue price of £1.50 per share and issue expenses were £1k, the transaction would be recorded in the balance sheet as follows:

SHAREHOLDERS' FUNDS	£k
Share capital	
Issued, 10,000 ordinary £1 shares	10
Reserves	
Share premium account	4*

*Share premium (£5k) less issuing expenses (£1k).

Under the dual aspect, the £14k of capital employed would be represented on the Assets side of the balance sheet as 'cash', pending translation into fixed assets or other items of working capital.

Share premium, then, represents the first type of shareholders' reserve. The second type of reserve relates to what appears to be a direct infringement of the 'historical cost' concept. As we have seen (Chapter 2), this concept enjoins that fixed assets be valued in the balance sheet at the cost of acquisition less accumulated depreciation. Through the process of depreciation, initial value is 'written down' and 'expensed' through the Profit and Loss Account. However, one category of fixed assets, land and buildings, has dispensation from such treatment. The reason is obvious. Property values, far from decreasing with age, have tended to increase over time, particularly when associated with development potential. But until the 1970s, such real estate was usually valued in the balance sheet at the cost of acquisition. In many cases, depreciation had been charged on buildings which occupied prime High Street sites. As a result, net assets were often represented at levels substantially below current values. In the predatory 1960s and early 1970s, such situations were prime targets for takeover at bargain-basement prices. Often there followed the process which has been variously described as 'asset stripping' (bad: unacceptable face of capitalism, etc.) or 'redeploying under-utilized assets' (good, regeneration of British industry, kicking and screaming into the twentieth century, etc.).

As a result, most firms now engage, on a regular basis, external specialists to revalue their property assets. On the Assets side of the balance sheet such a revaluation is recorded by increasing, or 'writing up', the value of the appropriate assets. The amount by which the value of the asset is increased – the surplus on revaluation – is shown on the Equities and Liabilities side of the balance sheet as a shareholders' reserve, 'Revaluation of Fixed Assets'. Hence if a firm's land and buildings stand in the books at a value of £1m but are revalued at £2m, fixed assets will be increased by £1m and a revaluation reserve created in the same amount.

The third type of shareholders' reserve, retained profit (or revenue reserve) has already been discussed. The amount which appears in this reserve reflects the profits which have been retained in the firm from its inception to the date of the balance sheet.

The share premium and revaluation reserves are classified as 'capital reserves'. As such they form part of the permanent capital of the firm and cannot be paid out in the form of dividend to ordinary shareholders. Retained profit, by contrast, is classified as a 'revenue reserve'. This reserve is available for distribution as dividend if considered appropriate by the directors of the company. If the current year's profit (after interest and tax) is insufficient to meet the recommended dividend, the balance may be taken from revenue reserve. If the company has incurred a loss and still wishes to pay a dividend, the whole amount will need to be derived from this reserve. Eyebrows will be raised in the City, mutterings will be heard about devouring seed-corn, but if the setback is temporary, recovery is underway and liquidity is high, the policy may be justified as a necessary boost to confidence. Such a policy may appear to reveal the unacceptable face of capitalism but is entirely within the firm's discretion.

Shareholders' funds, then, can be analyzed as follows:

Share Capital	*£k*
Issued	x
Reserves	
Share premium	x
Revaluation of fixed assets	x
Retained profit	x

The role of retained profit has already been discussed.

The amount of profit which a firm does retain, quite apart from the availability of profit, is obviously conditioned by its dividend policy. Dividend policy is a complex matter and involves shareholders' expectations as well as matters internal to the firm. Within the firm, liquidity, or the ability to find cash to pay a substantial dividend, could be a restraining factor. We are back to the dynamic cash model of the firm. If the Annual Report and Accounts show that the firm has made a profit, after interest and tax, of £100k, this does not mean that this amount is lying in readies in a bank vault while the directors ponder how much should go to shareholders, and how much should be reinvested in the firm. As we have seen, profit is not the same as cash generated. In addition, profit does not simply emerge at the year end: it is generated throughout the year and, insofar as it represents cash, is incorporated into the dynamic model and transformed into fixed assets and working capital. Liquidity, then, or the availability of cash, can be a determinant of dividend policy. Similarly, planned asset acquisition or the retirement of debt can pre-empt funds available for dividends. The operating environment can also influence dividend policy. If a firm operates in a cyclical environment, fat years and lean years, retentions in the upturn may be high to stabilize dividends in the downswings. In this situation, dividends in the trough of financial performance may well be topped up from retained profits.

The relationship of dividend to profit is usually expressed in the 'dividend cover' ratio:

$$\frac{\text{profit available for dividend}}{\text{dividend payable}}$$

If the firm, after tax and interest, turns in a profit of £5m and declares a dividend of £1m, the dividend is covered five times.

Shareholders' funds, or equity, comprise the first component of capital structure. The second component is made up of the long-term liabilities, or debt, of the firm. We are here mainly concerned with the firm's long-term borrowings. These loans may be secured or unsecured. If secured, the providers of the loan take priority, in a wind-up, over the providers of unsecured loans and other creditors. Security may relate to a specific asset or be vested in a floating charge on the generality of assets in the company.

Security can take many forms. We have already seen (Chapter 1) the copper-bottomed quality of Her Majesty's Government's security rating *vis à vis* the House of Rothschild in 1875. But, in more recent times, governments have been less than a stone-cold certainty in security terms. Indeed the Everest of debt raised by certain countries has led, in the banking parlours of the western world, to contemplation of an interesting philosophical question: 'Can a sovereign state go bankrupt?'

In 1981, thirty-two countries were in arrears on payment of interest and principal. In that year Poland defaulted. In 1982 Mexico defaulted to be followed, in 1983, by Brazil and Argentina. By early 1983, some $700b was owed to financial institutions and governments by various Eastern Bloc and developing countries. In 1985 Fidel Castro joined the debate: the debtor nations were acting humanely in removing a swelling from the wallets of the western world. The bankers demurred but an answer to the interesting philosophical question seemed to be emerging. The answer was 'No'! If you owe a bank $70 and can't repay, *you*'ve got problems. If you owe a bank $700b, and can't repay, the *bank*'s got problems. It has, in the argot, a surfeit of 'non-performing' assets. The dilemma is resolved by rescheduling the debts at escalating rates of interest.

Personal reputation can also be an overestimated source of security. In the 1920s and 1930s, Richard Whitney was head of the New York brokerage firm which bore his name. Straight from the top drawer of the eastern establishment, broker to the Olympian J. P. Morgan and Company, Whitney, as President of the New York Stock Exchange, came to embody Wall Street and high finance in the eyes of the American public. So it was that, in 1938, Richard Whitney, President of the Stock Exchange, approached with patrician tread a man drawn from a very different background, Bernard E. ('Sell 'em Ben') Smith, veteran market operator:

PRESIDENT OF THE NEW YORK STOCK EXCHANGE: 'Will you lend me $250k on my face?'

SELL 'EM BEN: 'You're putting a pretty high value on your face.'

The pitch was unsuccessful. Street wisdom triumphed over reputation. In truth, Whitney was in a financial fix. He had speculated to the hilt in the stock of an applejack firm, a beverage which he (and he alone) believed to be about to lubricate the parched palate of post-Prohibition America. Within weeks, Whitney's alternative sources of funds were revealed. He was charged and convicted of embezzling funds from the twin pillars of the establishment, the New York Yachting Club and the Stock Exchange Gratuity Fund. There's nowt so queer as folk.

In most cases, security needs to be specific and realizable. It can also be exotic. In Fourteen Hundred and Ninety-two Columbus sailed the Ocean Blue with funds raised by Queen Isabella of Spain on the security of her jewels. In more prosaic times, a building, a plot of land, item of equipment, backed up by a business plan, will serve just as well. The business plan (P & L Account, balance sheet, and, crucially, cash flow statement) will need to give the provider of the loan reassurance on:

  (i) the security of interest payments;
 (ii) the security of repayments of principal.

The security of interest payments is assessed from the 'interest cover'. This is measured as the ratio:

$$\frac{\text{profit before interest and tax}}{\text{interest payments}}$$

So, if the business plan indicates profits (before interest and tax) of £100k p.a. and interest payments are assessed at £10k p.a., the interest payments are covered ten times. The higher the cover, the greater the security. In our example, trading profit would need to fall by 90 per cent before interest payments were affected.

The other major indicator of security and solvency is the firm's 'debt ratio', measured as:

$$\frac{\text{long-term loans ('debt')}}{\text{long-term loans (+) shareholders' funds ('capital employed')}}$$

If a firm has net assets (fixed assets (+) working capital) of £2m and these net assets are resourced by shareholders' funds of £1.5m, and long-term loans of £0.5m, the debt ratio is:

$$\frac{£0.5m}{£0.5m + £1.5m} = 25\%$$

In other words, the book value of the firm's net assets would need to fall by 75 per cent before net assets ceased to cover the liabilities represented by the loans, a substantial margin of safety. The lower the debt ratio, the greater the security.

The debt ratio is important in understanding the financial workings of the firm. The ratio is usually termed the 'gearing' or 'leverage' of the firm. The higher the ratio, the higher the leverage. In the natural sciences, leverage is the effect produced by a straight horizontal bar, resting on a fulcrum, and used to raise a load at some point along its length by the application of a force at another point. The principle of leverage enables a large lifting effect to be produced by a relatively small force. In the financial metamorphosis of this principle, the force applied is the debt rate, the bar to which it is applied is profit, the fulcrum is the ratio of interest on loans, and the load to be lifted is return on shareholders' funds (equity). (Figure 17).

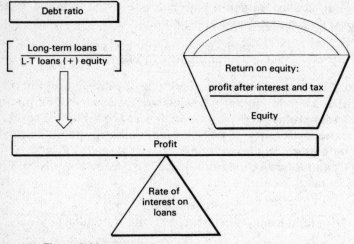

Figure 17: *Financial leverage*

To understand how the principles of financial leverage work, assume that we are setting up a company. We calculate that an initial investment of £100k will be required for fixed assets and working capital. But how much of this initial investment shall we raise in the form of debt, how much in equity? Let us assume that we have three options for our financial structure:

	Option 1 £k	Option 2 £k	Option 3 £k
Debt (long-term loans)	10	40	70
Equity (ordinary shares)	90	60	30

Interest on the long-term loans is fixed at 10 per cent. In all the options, we, the founders, would be putting up the equity in its entirety. The three options produce the following leverage:

Leverage (Debt Ratio)
%

Option 1	10
Option 2	40
Option 3	70

We estimate that in the first year of operation, profit, before interest and tax, will be £25k. The return on capital employed (profit before interest and tax (÷) capital employed) is, therefore, 25 per cent (£25/100k) for all three options. However, the return on *our* cash, the equity, is substantially different:

	Option 1 £k	Option 2 £k	Option 3 £k
Profit before tax and interest	25	25	25
Interest (at 10%)	1	4	7
Profit before tax	24	21	18
Tax (at, say, 50%)	12	10.5	9
Profit after tax	12	10.5	9
Equity	90	60	30
RETURN ON EQUITY (Profit after tax÷equity)	13.3%	17.5%	30%
DEBT RATIO	10%	40%	70%

The stronger the force applied in terms of the debt ratio, the greater the lift-off in terms of return on equity, and lift-off increases in geometric progression. In the case of the business start-up we have the added advantage under Option 3 that, for a modest outlay, we have maintained undiluted control of the company. All in all, Option 3 looks a nice little earner.

But, as usual, when everything in the financial garden looks lovely, in reality the wind is blowing weed spores over your hedge. The spores come in two forms. First, the providers of the loans will fail to see the justice in their receiving a measly 10 per cent return while we seem set fair to make 30 per cent on our grubstake. Having shared in the labour pains, they will be reluctant to see us walking off with the baby. Secondly, the same providers will know all about geometric progressions. A geometric series is a wondrous thing to behold in the ascendant. Unfortunately the descent is just as steep. A small reduction in profit can threaten interest payments. In brief, the higher the leverage, the higher the risk.

This risk is hinted at in the respective interest cover (profit before interest and tax ($\div$) interest payments) for the three options:

	Interest cover (times covered)	Debt ratio %
Option 1	25.00	10
Option 2	6.25	40
Option 3	3.57	70

And the downward realities of geometric progression, or reverse leverage, also contain risks for the equity holders if estimated profit fails to materialize. Let us assume that, in its first year of operation, our company made profits (before interest and tax) not of £25k but of only £8k:

	Option 1 £k	Option 2 £k	Option 3 £k
Debt	10	40	70
Equity	90	60	30
Capital Employed	100	100	100
Profit before interest and tax	8	8	8
Interest	1	4	7
Profit after interest	7	4	1
Tax	3.5	2	0.5
Profit after tax	3.5	2	0.5
Return on capital employed	8%	8%	8%
RETURN ON EQUITY	3.9%	3.3%	1.7%
Interest cover (times covered)	8	2	1.1
DEBT RATIO	10	40	70

We now see the ravages of reverse leverage. Although return on capital employed has dropped by 68 per cent, return on equity in the most highly leveraged option (3) has declined by 94 per cent. The lower the leverage, the smaller the fall in return on equity. In short, the effect of leverage is to cause return on equity to change more rapidly than return on capital employed. This effect is experienced both when profits are increasing and when they are declining. The higher the leverage, the greater the change. When things are good they are very, very good. When they're bad, they're horrid.

The leverage effect in the three options at both the higher (25 per cent on capital employed) and lower (8 per cent return) levels is shown below:

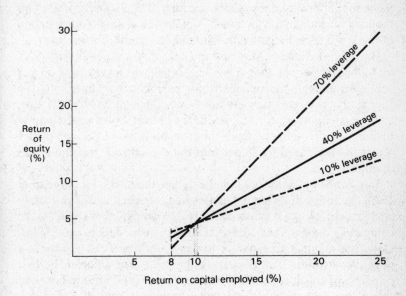

Figure 18: *Leverage effect*

When the return on capital employed exceeds the fulcrum rate of 10 per cent (the rate of interest on debt in our example), the more highly leveraged the option, the greater the return on equity. But when the return on capital employed drops below the rate of interest, reverse leverage comes into play. In our example, when return on capital employed is 8 per cent, the lowest leveraged option (1) provides the highest return on equity.

The workings of leverage, forward and reverse, were seen to spectacular effect on Wall Street in 1929. Share prices surged upwards in 1928 and early 1929. Loan finance was cheap and, apparently, limitless. Many highly leveraged investment companies were established to exploit the situation. Assume that such a company was set up at the end of May 1929 with capital of $100m, $70m in the form of debt, $30m as equity. The $100m brought into the firm is immediately invested in industrial shares. A proportion of those shares is lodged with the bank as security for the loan.

Between the end of May and the end of August 1929 the Index of Industrial Shares rose from 339 to 449, an increase of 30 per cent. Assuming that our portfolio performed in line with the Index, the company's assets are now valued at $130m. Of this, $70m is attributable to the providers of loans, $60m to the equity holders. In the space of three months the value of the company's assets has increased by 30 per cent but the value of the equity has doubled.

But Nemesis lurks behind the ticker-tape. By 13 November 1929, the Index of Industrial Shares had collapsed to 224, a drop of 50 per cent on its August peak. In ten weeks, the value of the company's assets has been reduced from $130m to $65m. Collateral against the loan is looking weak and the equity is a negative amount. If at that stage the bank had ignored the first principle of credit control ('in business there is no limit to how bad things can become') and avoided foreclosure, over the next two and a half years reverse leverage would have run riot. In July, 1932, the Index of Industrial Shares stood at 58.

Over the last thirty years many explanations have been tendered for the relatively poor performance of the British economy, full many a hand has been wrung over the 'English disease' of low pay, low productivity and low investment. The explanations have ranged from the grandiose (the wrath of God) to the gorblimey (a surfeit of fluoride and a deficiency of vitamins). The explanations have also shifted over time.

In the 1950s the received wisdom held that the nations vanquished in war had, somewhat unreasonably, derived a comparative advantage from having perforce to start from scratch on 'green-field' sites with new equipment and a motivated workforce. Moreover, as the sun set on the Empire, soft colonial markets were revealed to have bred a complacency which impaired the competitive thrust required to exploit new outlets. In the 1960s, the explanations became more pragmatic. British managers were unprofessional. The 'science of management', long understood by competitors, remained unexploited in the UK. Business schools, courses, degrees and diplomas were the answer. Politicians were too adversarial and governments distanced themselves from the horny-handed sons of toil in business and the trade unions. National plans, the National Economic Development Council and the corporate state were required. The system of industrial relations was based on conflict not consensus. Co-determination, tripartism and legislation were needed to replace strife. The scale of business was too small to exploit economies. Mergers were the solution.

In the 1970s, the educational system took a pasting – too few engineers and technologists, too many Arts graduates who, inconsiderately, grabbed the best jobs. The public sector came in for general obloquy: public sector muscling private sector out of money markets; taxes and social contributions soaking up GDP like blotting paper. Participation and social contracts would sort out industrial relations. Small was becoming beautiful and the notion of culture was emerging: Britain was an industrial nation which subscribed to pre-industrial values.

In the early 1980s, Harold Lever and George Edwards added to this galaxy of explanations. They suggested that leverage could be a prime cause of the disappointing performance of British industry in comparison with its competitors, particularly Japan and West Germany. They identified an 'Anglo-Saxon' tradition in the UK and older Commonwealth countries. In this tradition, the financial system was quite separate from the industrial system and, in the industrial system, high internal funding of investment, with low leverage, was the norm. If funding from internal sources was not available, many companies preferred not to invest rather than increase indebtedness. The policy was one of low debt and a leverage of around 30 per cent. If leverage was allowed to rise much higher there was a risk that, in a downturn, earnings would be consumed by interest payments with an inevitable effect on the stability of dividends. This 'safety first' attitude was contrasted with experience in Japan and West Germany. Here the financial and industrial systems were closely integrated and the major source of investment funds was long-term loans from the banks at very competitive rates of interest. In 1975, the average leverage of industrial and commercial companies in Japan was 85 per cent. Such levels produced a potentially high level of financial risk but, paradoxically, a low level of business risk. Given the availability of low cost, long-term loans and the smartness with which Japanese managers invested these funds in assets, the earnings flowing from the assets easily covered interest payments and the surplus provided funds which, with more loans, generated further growth. A virtuous circle was created, in which the threat of reverse leverage was remote. Lever and Edwards suggested that investment in the UK might be lagging simply because UK industry did not have access to the low-cost external funds available to foreign competitors.

The argument has considerable merit. However, even if UK industry did have such access, the funds would have to be consistently invested in assets which provided large enough returns to meet interest payments, provide dividends and contribute to future growth. Availability of funds is important but the smartness with which these funds are invested is paramount. It is time to turn our attention to capital investment decisions.

7. Capital Investment Decisions – Theory

'Si monumentum requiras, circumspice.' ('If you seek a monument, look around.')
Inscription in honour of Sir Christopher Wren, St Paul's Cathedral

In linguistic philosophy there is a category of propositions which are 'necessary' but not 'sufficient'. Hence, abstinence from cigarette smoking is held to be *necessary* for good health but such abstinence, in itself, is not *sufficient* to ensure the desired result. In the semantics of finance, capital investment decisions conform to this category of proposition. High investment does not guarantee corporate growth but an insufficiency of investment is often the harbinger of low, slow or no growth. Obviously you don't hit the jackpot unless you insert coins in the machine, but the micro-circuitry of the machine, like life, brooks no smooth correlation between coinage inserted and jackpots attained. The quality of the decisions made, not the amount invested, is the key to corporate growth. It's not the size of the conjuror's wand that puts the rabbit in the hat but the magic of the performer. Capital investment appraisal techniques attempt to provide insight into this magic.

Capital investment decisions involve consideration of two major variables:

  (i) cash
  (ii) time

A decision to invest in the acquisition of fixed assets necessitates a commitment of cash now or in the near future in the expectation of gains in the more distant future. But there is no such thing as a free

119

lunch. The cash committed carries with it a cost. If the cash is borrowed or raised from a share issue, cost comes in the form of interest payments, dividends, issue expenses etc. There are also implications for liquidity. Even if the cash stems from retained earnings, there is still an opportunity cost. There is always an alternative use. The cash could have been invested outside the firm at a rate of interest or elsewhere within the firm at a rate of return.

The time dimension brings with it a context rich in uncertainty. In logic, the further away the putative gains are, the greater the uncertainty which attaches to their realization. But logic can vie with emotion: in human nature the more distant the object, the more attractive the appearance – distance lends enchantment. When the planning horizon of the investment project is necessarily long, decisions taken and cash invested now can take aeons of time before fructifying and producing benefits. In April 1985, the Seikan Tunnel was opened: thirty-two miles long, it linked the Japanese islands of Hokkaido and Honshu. Work had started twenty-one years earlier. The decision to proceed had been reached in the early 1960s. Underground coal mines, power stations and petrochemical complexes involve gestation periods of at least a decade. Decisions taken in such contexts are reversible only with the loss of much cash and *amour propre*. Decisions made within long-term planning horizons can make or break companies. Rolls Royce and RB211 is an example of the latter. But a decision not to invest can have equally parlous consequences: recent aversion to investing in the production of video-recorders has cost several British companies dear.

The fundamental problem is that life must be lived forwards but can only be understood in retrospect. In 1960, in the field of micro-electronics, the simplest functional circuit needed two transistors and at least five other components. By the late 1970s, twenty thousand functions could be contained on a single silicon chip. In two decades the cost of an electronic function had been reduced by a factor of one thousand. But could this have been foreseen in 1960, as the princes of industry paced up and down and soliloquized – 'to invest or not to invest'? Hindsight is the only perfect science. Even where the gestation period is short and the market mature, capital investment decisions are crucial in shaping the future contours of the firm. Given that our nightmares are more vivid than our dreams it is not surprising that many firms, when faced with a key investment decision, suffer a state of corporate nervous breakdown. Investment appraisal techniques do not remove the uncertainty but attempt to set it in context by evaluating the implications of decisions in terms of cash and time.

The detail of capital investment projects differs from product to product, industry to industry. But the objectives which such projects are designed to achieve conform to a relatively simple typography. In terms of objectives, projects are usually concerned with one or a combination of the following:

(a) Expansion

At its simplest, an expansionary project is designed to increase the output of a product or service which the firm is already providing: uncertainty is reduced if the route to expansion lies through technology and fixed assets which are familiar to the firm and if the target is a familiar market. Here the firm is 'sticking to the knitting' but increasing its output of woolly jumpers. Typical examples are additional plant, offices and retail outlets which replicate, without replacing, existing facilities. An element of uncertainty is introduced if the replication is to take place in hitherto virgin territory, for example Nissan's automobile plant at Washington, Co. Durham. The incidence of uncertainty increases if the firm is expanding through diversification even though the assets and the technology are familiar: synergy's siren song led Trust House Forte into the travel business with disappointing results: in many cases two plus two turns out to equal not five but three, if you're lucky. Uncertainty increases still further if the expansion is designed to take the firm into new products and services on the back of unfamiliar technology and assets: early indications are that Sinclair Vehicles' C5 (electronic car) project conforms to this type.

(b) Replacement

Fixed assets, with the exception of land, have a finite life. Depreciation theory teaches that, at some stage, the asset will become 'time-served' and will require replacement. But like is rarely replaced with like. Steam locomotives are replaced by diesels which in turn are displaced by electrification. Technological advance implies that the replacement contains benefits in the form of reduced cost and enhanced quality. Replacement can also bring with it an element of expansion: the replacement, through scaling up or operational improvement, can provide greater capacity than the replaced asset. Conversely, many expansionist projects contain an element of replacement. Development of a new plant on a green-field site can incorporate the replacement and closure of existing plants and still provide the firm with increased capacity. In the 1970s, the barrelage of numerous small, local breweries was subsumed in the capacity of the new expansionary, centralized facilities of the Big Brewers in the UK. Given the pace of technological advance, policy on asset replacement can no longer be a reactive decision to the passage of time. Plant and equipment may be operating sweetly and have several years to go to retirement age, but if an alternative is available which, in military parlance, gives more bangs to the buck, then a policy of asset euthanasia must be considered. Apart from technological factors, the workings of the market may demand positive decisions. In the aftermath of the Yom Kippur War (October, 1973) the price of oil increased by a factor of five. The economics of oil utilization were radically altered and the change was later reinforced by the Iranian Revolution (1979). Oil-fired industrial boilers lost their comparative cost advantage over other fuels, particularly coal. Although many industrial boiler units were far from time-expired, reboilering to consume coal offered considerable cost-reduction. In this, and many similar replacement decisions, the benefit is measured not in increased sales but in reduced costs.

(c) Statutory requirements

'Frontier capitalism' began to be trammelled in the UK in the nineteenth century. Factories Acts laid down minimum standards of welfare and safety while the developing science of occupational medicine began to establish minimum standards of industrial health. Expanding knowledge and rising expectations lead to the continual updating of these standards, often at considerable capital cost. More recently, consumerism and the environmental revolution have led to the introduction of new standards on subjects as diverse as food additives and foul-water emissions. Again, capital investment on a mandatory basis is usually required to achieve compliance. The 'assertive society' and increased 'corporate social responsibility' will ensure a continuation of the process and, in the complex 'global village', the costs can be astronomical. Smoke emission was first controlled in the UK by the Alkali Act of 1906. Clean Air Acts followed in the 1950s. In the 1970s, the acidification of lakes in Scandinavia and tree loss in Germany produced the hypothesis that emissions might have damaging effects at great distances from source and at relatively low concentrations. 'Acid rain' was discovered. It was suggested that a major cause of the environmental damage in northern Europe was emission of sulphur dioxide from tall-stack, coal-burning power stations in the UK. By 1984, environmental concern had been incorporated into draft EEC proposals which envisaged a 60 per cent reduction in sulphur dioxide emissions by 1995. To achieve this reduction, flue-gas desulphurization 'scrubbers' would need to be installed at the major coal-burning power stations. The Central Electricity Generating Board estimated the capital cost at £1,500m. It may appear that capital investment appraisal techniques are irrelevant where the expenditure is mandatory. However, alternative routes may be available to achieve the mandatory objective. For example, sulphur dioxide emissions might be reduced by attempting to reduce the sulphur content of the input coal. Or the reduction might be achieved by diminished generation from coal-fired stations and an increased reliance on nuclear generation. Where the objective is mandatory, the decision is not so much 'do/no do' but 'how do'. Investment appraisal techniques assist in isolating the most cost-effective route.

Capital investment decisions, then, when concerned with expansion or replacement, involve the commitment of cash now, or in the near future, to secure benefits in the more distant future. Investment appraisal techniques are designed to assist decision-makers answer the three key questions about a project:

(a) Is it *worthwhile* to the firm to invest in the project? Investment appraisal answers the question by relating the anticipated financial benefits of the project to its anticipated financial costs. The answer is couched in purely financial terms. The benefits and the costs are limited to those which accrue within the financial territory of the firm. 'Externalities' are excluded: a green-field development creates both social costs and social benefits – visual intrusion, noise, traffic as well as employment, direct and indirect. Investment appraisal takes no cognisance of such externalities except insofar as they enter the firm's financial territory as costs associated with planning conditions and statutory requirements, or as benefits associated with government grants. In the territory of finance, it is possible to render separate accounts to God and to Caesar.

(b) Which, among mutually exclusive projects, is it *more worthwhile* for the firm to adopt? As we have seen, in many cases, the objectives of a project can be reached by a variety of routes. An item of plant or equipment may be capable of replacement by a plethora of alternatives, each with different profiles of financial cost and benefit. Expansion in a familiar market may be achieved by in-house development or by the acquisition of a competitor. In such cases, investment appraisal is concerned with identifying which of the alternatives is *more* worthwhile to the firm.

(c) Where the total amount of finance available for capital investment is limited to a finite sum for a specified period, and the total cost of projects 'on offer' exceeds this sum, which mix of projects is it *most worthwhile* for the firm to adopt? In the common situation of capital rationing, invest-ment appraisal provides a financial ranking mechanism with the total amount of funds available acting as the cut-off point.

So what does all this mean in concrete terms? Concrete Terms PLC is a company operating in the cement and gravel business. Demand for its product exceeds the capacity of existing plant and machinery. The company estimates that the installation of an additional processing unit, operating at full capacity, will absorb this excess demand. An expansionary project, using familiar technology and aimed at an existing market, is born. The first key question is asked. Is the implementation of such a project worthwhile to the firm?

At this stage four variables enter the equation of worthwhileness:

   (i) the installed cost of the unit and the time taken for installation
  (ii) the anticipated useful life of the unit
 (iii) for each year of useful life, the estimated changes in the firm's cash inflow and outflow resulting directly from the installation of the additional unit. The unit will generate extra sales which will increase cash inflow. But the unit will require additional labour and will consume additional raw materials, electricity, etc. Cash outflow will increase. Less obvious implications should be included in the cash outflow. If installation of the unit will lead to increased overheads (additional maintenance staff, expanded canteen facilities to accommodate the extra personnel, additional supervisory staff, etc.), the increase is a direct result of the project and should be reflected in the cash outflow. Also included should be the effect of the project on working capital (increased stocks and debtors offset by increased creditors). Investment allowances and taxation should be taken into account. Since the calculation is solely concerned with cash movements, depreciation should be ignored
  (iv) terminal value of the machine: the re-sale or scrap value of the unit at the end of its useful life

In our example, the installed cost of the unit is £90k. Installation is estimated to be completed one month after placing the order for the unit. The useful life of the machine is assessed at three years. Annual cash inflows and outflows which result directly from the installation are estimated as follows:

	Cash Inflow £k	Cash Outflow £k	Net Cash Flow £k
Year 1	80	(35)	45
Year 2	80	(35)	45
Year 3	75	(45)	30

The terminal value of the machine at the end of its useful life is assessed at £1k. This represents its sale for scrap and is included in the cash inflow shown above for Year 3.

To assess the worthwhileness of the project, we need to find a way of expressing the relationship of the net cash flows which emanate *from* the project (column 3 above) to the initial outlay (£90k) entailed *by* the project. The full project cash flow is as follows:

	Cash Inflow £k	Cash Outflow £k	Net Cash Flow £k
Initial outlay	—	(90)	(90)

As a result of this outlay

	Cash Inflow £k	Cash Outflow £k	Net Cash Flow £k
Year 1	80	(35)	45
Year 2	80	(35)	45
Year 3	75	(45)	30
		Total net cash flow	120
		LESS Initial outlay	(90)
		Net benefit	30

It appears, then, that, for an initial outlay of £90k, £120k will be earned, a net benefit of £30k. This represents a 33⅓ per cent rate of return, over a three-year period, on an investment of £90k.

Annualize the rate of return, compare it with our cost of capital and . . . the result will be as useful as a chocolate teapot.

As we have said earlier, capital investment decisions involve not only considerations of cash but also of time. The assessment of worthwhileness is concerned not only with the magnitude of the cash flows but also with the phasing of these flows. Worthwhileness depends not just on the amount of benefit received but also on when that benefit was received. The time dimension must be taken into account. We must grapple with the 'time-value theory of money'.

Consider the cash flows which arise from our project. Assume that the cash flow benefit materializes at the end of each year. The net cash flow in Year 1, at £45k, is identical to the net cash flow in Year 2. But if we were offered a choice, £45k in the hand in twelve months' time or £45k in our palm in twenty-four months, which would we take? We would take £45k in twelve months' time. At the very least we could reinvest this sum at a rate of interest before the second option became due. If we assume an interest rate of 10 per cent per annum, the first £45k would be worth £49½k before the second £45k became due. If this time dimension is introduced, we reach the conclusion that identical amounts of cash which arise in different years do not have the same value to us now. The sooner the cash arises, the greater the opportunities for reinvestment at a rate of interest or a rate of return. This, in essence, is the 'time-value theory of money'. It follows that, in the assessment of worthwhileness, future cash flows need to be adjusted for the time factor and reduced to a common value base. The value base used is the amount which future sums are worth to us now, the 'present value' (PV). The route to the determination of PV lies through the process of discounting. The result is termed 'discounted cash flow' (DCF).

Most people are familiar with the technique of compounding. Compounding calculates what a present sum will be worth at a future date at a given rate of interest. Compounding is concerned with terminal values:

	Amount £	Compound Interest (10%) £	Terminal Value £
Now	1.00	—	—
12 months' time	1.00	0.10	1.10
24 months' time	1.00	0.21	1.21

£1 receivable now is preferable to an identical sum receivable in twelve or twenty-four months because of the reinvestment potential. At a 10 per cent rate of interest, a sum of £1 now is the same as a sum of £1.10 receivable in twelve months' time or £1.21 receivable in twenty-four months' time. Compounding is concerned with terminal values.

Discounting reverses the process and concerns itself not with terminal values but with present values. If we assume a 10 per cent rate of interest, compounding shows that £1 now is worth £1.10 receivable in twelve months' time. Discounting calculates what £1, receivable in twelve months' time, is worth to us now, in other words the PV of £1 receivable in twelve months' time at a rate of interest of 10 per cent. The PV is:

$$£ \frac{1.00}{1.10} = £0.909$$

Similarly, the PV of £1 receivable in two years' time at a rate of interest of 10 per cent is :

$$£ \frac{1.00}{1.21} = £0.826$$

In other words, £1 receivable in twelve months' time is worth 90.9p to us now while £1 receivable in twenty-four months' time is worth 82.6p to us now if we assume an interest rate of 10 per cent. The technique can easily be checked. If we invest £0.826 now, compound interest will increase it to £1 in twenty-four months' time:

	£
Investment now	0.826
First year's interest (10%)	0.083
After 12 months	0.909
Second year's interest (10%)	0.091
	1.00

Discount factors come in pre-calculated tables as shown at Appendix 1. At the side of the columns are the rates of interest, along the top, the years. So, if we want the discount factor for a 10 per cent rate of interest on a sum arising in Year 1, we move to the row headed 10 per cent and the column Year 1. The discount factor is 0.909 (as calculated above). Similarly, the discount factor for Year 2 at the rate of interest is 0.826 (as above). A glance at the table will show that, whatever the rate of interest, the further away the receipt of an identical sum of money, the lower its PV. At a 10 per cent rate of interest, £1 receivable ten years hence is worth £0.386 to us now. The technique of discounting enables the time-value theory of money to be incorporated into the assessment of worthwhileness. But understanding the theory of Discounted Cash Flow is like assembling flat-pack furniture – you don't often get it together at the first attempt. So, in an attempt to put the theory into practice, let's return to our example.

We already have estimates of the four variables in the equation of worthwhileness – capital cost, useful life, annual net cash flows and terminal value. To apply the process of discounted cash flow one further variable is required: the appropriate rate of interest at which to discount the cash flows. The rate selected is designed to reflect the firm's cost of capital. It should reflect:

  (i) the cost of borrowing if the project is to be financed by additional debt;

  (ii) the cost of equity capital, including issue expenses, if a share issue is to provide the funds;

(iii) opportunity cost if retained earnings are the source of funds: in other words, the rate of interest at which the funds could be loaned outside the firm or the rate of return on alternative uses within the firm.

In many cases, a composite figure is used. Assume that a 10 per cent cost of capital is indicated. We have now assembled all the variables in the equation.

Under the conventions of DCF, the year of installation equates to the present and is termed 'Year 0'. Subsequent cash flows are assumed to arise at the end of the relevant year. Our project can now be evaluated.

		Net Cash Flow £	Discount Factor (10%)	Discounted Cash Flow £
Year 0	*Initial outlay.*	(90,000)	—	(90,000)
Year 1		45,000	0.909	40,905
Year 2		45,000	0.826	37,170
Year 3		30,000	0.751	22,530
			Gross present value	100,605
			LESS Initial outlay	(90,000)
			Net present value	10,605

Through the application of the discount factor, the cash flows, whenever in the future they arise, are converted to the common value base of PV and indicate what they are worth to us now. The cash flows in Years 1–3 are, therefore, now denominated in the same value terms and can be added to give the project's gross present value. The initial outlay, since it will take place in present time, is already expressed in PV and can, legitimately, be subtracted from the gross present value. The result is the project's 'net present value' (NPV). The NPV demonstrates the financial worthwhileness to the firm of the project after meeting the appropriate cost of capital. If the NPV is positive, undertaking the project will increase the firm's wealth by the amount of the NPV. If the NPV is negative, the project cannot cover the firm's cost of capital and implementation will lead to a diminution in the firm's wealth to the extent of the negative NPV.

A positive NPV, in a risk-free project, provides an affirmative answer to the first key question – 'Is it worthwhile?' The greater the positive NPV, the greater the worthwhileness. However, the NPV is expressed in sterling terms. The more comprehensive index of worthwhileness is the percentage rate of return which, when compared with the cost of capital, can indicate not only worthwhileness but also the extent of the worthwhileness. The DCF 'internal rate of return' (IRR) takes up where NPV leaves off and provides such quantification. The IRR represents that rate of interest which discounts the cash flows of the project, including the initial outlay, to an NPV of zero. The appropriate rate of interest/ discount factor can be found by trial and error. In our example, discounting at the cost of capital (10 per cent) produced a substantial, positive NPV. This indicates that the IRR is well in excess of 10 per cent. So, try a discount factor of 20 per cent (Appendix 1). Remember, the purpose is to discover that discount factor which produces an NPV of zero:

		Net Cash Flow £	Discount Factor (20%)	Discounted Cash Flow £
Year 0	*Initial outlay*	(90,000)	—	(90,000)
Year 1		45,000	0.833	37,485
Year 2		45,000	0.694	31,230
Year 3		30,000	0.579	17,370
			Gross present value	86,085
		LESS	Initial outlay	(90,000)
			Net present value	(3,915)

The negative NPV demonstrates that the project cannot sustain a cost of capital as high as 20 per cent. The discount factor which produces a zero NPV must lie somewhere between 10 and 20 per cent. The approximate rate can be found by interpolation:

			Differences
Discount Factor (%)	10	20	10
NPV (£)	10,605	(3,915)	14,520

Interpolation suggests that the appropriate rate is 17 per cent.

$$10\% \; (+) \left(\frac{10605}{14520} \times 10\% \right) = 17\%$$

This can be checked by application to the example:

		Net Cash Flow £	Discount Factor (17%)	Discounted Cash Flow £
Year 0	*Initial outlay*	(90,000)	—	—
Year 1		45,000	0.854	38,430
Year 2		45,000	0.730	32,850
Year 3		30,000	0.624	18,720
			Gross present value	90,000
		LESS	Initial outlay	(90,000)
			Net present value	—

The project, then, has an internal rate of return of 17 per cent. This means that if the project were financed by an overdraft type loan, at 17 per cent interest, it could exactly meet repayments of interest and principal:

Year	Capital Outstanding on Project £	ADD Interest at 17% £	Total Debt at year end £	LESS Repayments from Cash Flow £	Closing Balance £
1	90,000	15,300	105,300	(45,000)	60,300
2	60,300	10,300	70,600	(45,000)	25,600
3	25,600	4,400	30,000	(30,000)	—

Since the cost of capital is only 10 per cent, the message of the positive NPV is reinforced. The project, if risk free, is eminently worthwhile to the firm. The first key question is answered.

Now for the second key question. The project is deemed to be worthwhile but can the objectives of the project, expansion to absorb excess demand, be achieved by a route which is *more* worthwhile to the firm? Assume that an alternative unit is available with a higher efficiency than the unit evaluated in the example. The capital cost is £160k with installation one month after placing the order. Useful life is estimated at three years. Net cash flows are assessed as follows:

	£k
Year 1	80
Year 2	70
Year 3	50

Terminal value, included in Year 3's cash flow, is estimated at £5k. Is investment in Unit 2 more worthwhile than investment in Unit 1? First, the NPV of Unit 2 is calculated using the firm's cost of capital (10 per cent).

		Net Cash Flow *£*	*Discount Factor* *(10%)*	*Discounted Cash Flow* *£*
Year 0	*Initial outlay*	(160,000)	—	(160,000)
Year 1		80,000	0.909	72,720
Year 2		70,000	0.826	57,820
Year 3		50,000	0.751	37,550
			Gross present value	168,090
			LESS Initial outlay	160,000
			Net present value	8,090

The NPV, though positive, is less than that achieved by the first unit. The IRR is lower, at 13 per cent (calculated by interpolation).

133

Unit 1, then, provides a worthwhile investment opportunity to the firm. Its IRR at 17 per cent is well above the cost of capital at 10 per cent. In addition, it provides a more worthwhile investment opportunity than Unit 2, whose IRR is only 13 per cent.

But is the installation of Unit 1 part of the mix of projects which it is *most* worthwhile for the firm to undertake? Assume that the firm has taken a policy decision to limit funds available for capital expenditure to £300k in the forthcoming year. No mandatory projects to conform with legislation are anticipated. The cost of capital is assessed at 10 per cent. In this situation of capital rationing, projects with returns higher than the cost of capital have no guarantee of acceptance. They are competing with each other for limited resources. A ranking mechanism can be established by using comparative IRRs. The amount available (£300k) represents the cut-off point:

PROJECT TITLE	Capital cost £k	IRR %	Cumulative Capital Cost £k
Expansion, product A	30	24	30
New distribution outlet	100	21	130
Acquisition, product B	80	19	210
Expansion, product C*	90	17	300
--- CUT OFF			
Re-boilering, main factory	100	14	400

*our project

The techniques of discounted cash flow, then, take into account not only considerations of cash but also the dimension of time. Future cash flows are translated into a common currency, present value. If the net present value is positive, *prima facie* it is worthwhile for the firm to undertake that project. The internal rate of return uses the same currency to indicate the return in a form easily comparable with the cost of capital.

The techniques take some understanding but, once mastered, provide a comprehensive framework for the evaluation of investment projects. Unfortunately, there is no short cut to such a mastery. To seek one is as futile as looking for an easy route up the north wall of the Eiger.

8. Capital Investment Decisions – Practice

'When things go wrong, everything is a mistake'.
Shah of Persia, in exile

The techniques of discounted cash flow fit snugly into a view of management as one vast logic diagram, an analytical game of quantified ladders and identified snakes, a technified component of a wider world made safe for reason, logic and analysis (Figure 19). The managers who inhabit this world operate with a rationality so cool that a little light comes on whenever they open their mouths. In this world a firm optimizes its capital investment. It continues to invest so long as its marginal return on investment exceeds its marginal cost of capital. In this way the net present value of the firm is maximized. Goals are set and missions defined, environments are beadily scanned, opportunities are isolated and projects identified. A spot of quantification and into the DCF machine the project goes. Then, snakes duly avoided, it's simply a question of implementing, monitoring and commissioning with a little cracker-barrel philosophy along the way – making two blades of grass grow where only one grew before, acorns into oak trees, longest marches starting with first steps. Strike up the band! We have strayed into the Theatre of Management which gave us such memorable productions as 'High-Rise Flats', 'Big is Beautiful' and 'Instant Coffee in Plastic Cups'.

We are back to linguistic philosophy and propositions which are necessary but not sufficient. Techniques like DCF which rely on logic, reason and analysis are very necessary if sound investment decisions are to be taken. But the simple application of the techniques is not sufficient to ensure the soundness of the decisions. Sufficiency is approached if, in applying the techniques, two caveats are noted:

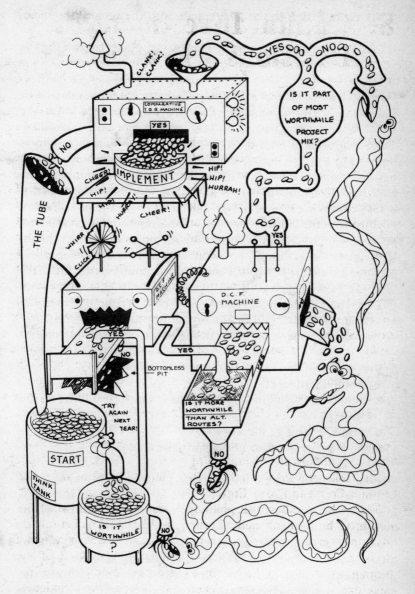

Figure 19: *The logic machine*

    (i) do not confuse the appearance with the reality, the menu with the meal;

   (ii) do not confuse a part of management with the whole, the waves with the tide.

First, appearance and reality. Capital investment proposals usually slide onto the decision-maker's desk in neatly packaged form. The variables are assembled in orderly fashion and duly quantified. Time is a series of lines on a bar chart. Myriad human activity is reduced to a single entity, the NPV or IRR. The whole, decked out with market research, artist's impressions, photomontages and scale models, has about it a patina of determinism and certainty. It is easy to confuse the menu with the meal, to see the prize but not the dust. But the reality is that the values attached to the variables, however sophisticated the derivation, are no more than estimates. If the premise is flawed, no amount of scientific technique will produce a conclusion which is sound. In computerspeak, GIGO! – Garbage In, Garbage Out – with its corollary BOTTOMS – Back On To The Old Manual System. Now consider the possibility of erroneous estimates in a major capital investment project. Look no further than the variables in the equation of worthwhileness:

- capital cost and installation or construction period
- useful life of asset
- annual cash inflows and outflows which result from the project
- terminal value of the asset
- the appropriate discount factor to be applied

Capital cost and completion time are notoriously prone to error where new technology is involved. The Sydney Opera House was intended to put Australia on the cultural map and to dispel for good the raw image of 'ockerism'. As befitted such a prestigious project and so noble an aim, the design was put out to international competition. The futuristic design submitted by the little-known Danish architect, Jorn Utzon, was duly awarded the palm. The design included several architectural features unknown to existing constructional technology. No matter. Estimates were made, and in 1957 it was announced that by 1962, New South Wales would have the finest opera house in the solar system at a cost of $A7m. In the event, the building was finally completed in 1972 at a cost of $A102m. Ironically, completion was only achieved in 1972 by designing out some of the most innovatory features. Indeed, so radical was the re-design that opera was relegated to a subsidiary auditorium too small for the more expansive productions.

Projects designed not to apply new technology but to 'scale-up' or adapt existing technology, can also involve mind-wrenching problems of quantification. Stripped to its essentials, the Concorde project was designed to transfer the technology of supersonic flight from military to civil aviation, 'swords into ploughshares'. In the springtime of the project, the early 1960s, estimates envisaged a project cost of £150m–£170m with a market for 400 planes. In the event, sixteen planes were built and nine were sold, all to the national airlines of the project's progenitors. The total project cost was around £2,000m.

Mother Nature can also emerge as an unpitying foe, particularly to grandiose agricultural and civil engineering projects. In 1947, in the age of austerity, the British Government started a scheme to turn 3½m acres of Tanzanian bush into a major source of high-protein food, to wit, the humble groundnut. In the event, more nuts were bought as seed than were produced as food. Attempts to turn the Sudan into the 'bread-bowl of Africa' and the Amazonian rain forests in to an agribusiness of fast-growing timber have met similar opposition. Beware, also, projects which involve the artistic temperament. Poetic licence comes expensive. The story, no doubt apocryphal, is told of Lord Grade poring over the finances of his film *Raise the Titanic*. 'It would have been cheaper,' he sighs, 'to have lowered the Atlantic.'

Projects which, in terms of capital cost and completion time, turn sour can become the Bermuda Triangle of the financial world. Vast amounts of cash and time disappear with no hope of rescue. When things do start to fall apart, odd phenomena occur. The less the progress, the thicker the Progress Reports and, whatever stage the project reaches, the cost to completion remains the same. An awesome decision now looms – to cut or to compound. To cut your losses, abort the project and face your bankers and shareholders with an eggy visage. Or to convince yourself that flowers can grow in a weed-patch, to continue and risk compounding your losses. To abort a major project is probably the hardest and bravest decision a firm can make.

After the oil-price hike of 1974, Shell, like most of its sister oil companies, decided to increase its rate of diversification. Energy futurologists pointed to an energy future based on Coconuc – coal, conservation and nuclear power. Shell expanded into coal. It also entered the nuclear field. Jointly with the American firm General Dynamics, Shell began to develop a pressurized water reactor in the USA. By the late 1970s the joint venture had consumed substantial funds and the return remained illusory. Shell quietly and bravely cut its losses and withdrew. It is less easy for governments to display similar flexibility. Concorde, De Lorean, Lear Fan . . . only when the solids are positively hitting the punkah is the decision to cut taken.

But, occasionally, very occasionally, the odds are confounded and the one-legged man wins the backside-kicking contest. In the 1860s David Davies of Llandinam was convinced that high-grade steam-coal lay beneath a sylvan Welsh valley, its river aleap with salmon. So he set about the laborious and expensive process of sinking shafts to prove the measures of coal. Much shafting, no measures. Much cash outflow, no cash inflow. Moment of destiny. Men due to be paid, resources down to half a crown. Time for Davies to come clean. Direct communication with workforce. 'OK,' say workforce, with nice mixture of idealism and opportunism, 'give us the half-crown and we'll work on.' Two weeks later coal was struck. The valley was the Rhondda. Within twenty years, the Rhondda was the centre of the international coal trade and Cardiff, by tonnage, was the second largest port in the world. By 1913, the Rhondda had fifty-eight collieries and 40,000 colliers. David Davies made a fortune and founded a dynasty. But such examples are as rare as rocking-horse manure.

There can, then, be unforeseen difficulties in bringing a project on stream within approved limits of cost and time. But even if the 'day late, dollar short' syndrome can be avoided, the second variable in the equation of worthwhileness – the useful life of the asset – lurks in wait. Once brought on stream, for how long will the asset continue to yield its cash benefits? In the last two decades, technological development has been a major foreshortener of asset life. In the 1940s, 80 per cent of the world's watches came from Switzerland. By the 1980s, Swiss market share had been reduced to 20 per cent. 'Clockwork' had been displaced by quartz systems and integrated circuits while the supple fingers of the assembly workers had replaced the traditional skills of the workbench. Apart from technology, tastes may change and the asset be confined to the lumber room of yesterday's enthusiasms – skateboard parks, ten-pin bowling alleys, cinemas and music-halls. Good taste may even re-emerge and confound the baleful notion that nobody ever got rich by over-estimating the public's taste. Real ale, fresh-baked bread, stone-ground flour, free-range eggs may be demanded when you've committed investment to the nastier alternatives. Legislation, regulation and harmonization can intrude – sweeteners, colourants, asbestos, and Golden Delicious apples.

Or you can tread on the rake of politics. In the mid 1970s, Chrysler (UK) won a much-acclaimed order to supply Avenger cars in kit form to an Iran ruled by a technocratic Shah. Due investment was made in plant and equipment at Chrysler's plant in Coventry. Come the Iranian Revolution of 1979 and the Fundamentalism of the mullahs rated the prayer-mat more highly than the internal combustion engine. The political influence may be more tangential. In the early 1980s, John Brown Engineering won a contract worth £104m to supply turbines to the Siberian gas-pipeline. The turbines were manufactured by John Brown in the UK under licence from the General Electric Company of America. Appropriate investment was made by John Brown. Meanwhile, in the Gdansk shipyards the word 'solidarity' was assuming new significance. By 1983, Poland was in turmoil. In response President Reagan embargoed the export of US high technology to the Soviet Union. For a time John Brown was impaled on the horns of a dilemma. Should it respect the licensing agreement with GE and face heavy penalities from the Soviet Union for non-delivery? Or should it fulfil its contract with the Soviet Union and sour the American connection? The choice was like that given to the condemned man in the electric chair. Do you want AC or DC?

Even more simply the project may come on stream when the world needs its benefits as badly as a goldfish needs a motor-cycle. In an early stirring of the service sector, the British Tourist Board was established in the 1930s to attract tourists from abroad to Britain. It duly laid plans to open bureaux in the major capitals of Western Europe. It opened its Berlin bureau in 1939.

Even if the project can be steered safely between the Scylla of capital cost/installation time and the Charybdis of useful asset life, the third variable, annual cash flows generated by the project, remains to be negotiated. The difficulties are obvious.

On the cash inflow side, estimates of revenue depend, inter alia, on assumptions about market size, share and growth. These in turn depend on the decisions of competitors, present and potential, at home and abroad. And the whole dish is garnished with assumptions on macro-economic factors, national and trans-national. At the one extreme the firm can set its face against over-sophistication and rely upon Say's Law, 'supply creates its own demand'. Faced with a projection which shows falling income levels among customers, it can find solace in the Duesenberry Effect: 'when income declines consumption is not cut symmetrically with the increase in consumption when income was rising'. At the other extreme the firm can attempt to predict in detail the kind of world upon which its product or service will be launched when the project bears fruit. The firm can rely, in its predictions, on Kitchin Cycles, thirty-nine months in length, conditioned by fluctuations in business stock-levels. Or it can rely on Juglar Cycles, seven to eight years in length, dependent on business investment in plant and equipment. Or it can embrace Kuznets Cycles, twenty years in length, induced by population changes and house-building. Or it can go for the daddy of them all, Kondratiev Cycles, forty years in length, the function of major inventions. But, even with a cornucopia of market research and econometric analysis, you still don't see the bullet that's going to kill you, the 'displacement factor', the shock to the system which turns the constants into variables, when oil is no longer $2 a barrel and the Lebanon ceases to be the Switzerland of the Middle East.

The cash outflow side is prone to many of the above influences.

In addition, estimates of cash outflow depend on projected levels of operational efficiency. How much is it going to cost, on an annual basis, to work the assets created by the project? And here the human factor begins to intrude. Most of us are all in favour of progress so long as it doesn't involve change. But projects inevitably involve change. How will people react? British business history is pitted with projects where the actual reaction differed greatly from the estimate. Installation of photo composition, facsimile transmission and web-offset printing facilities in the newspaper industry has often been followed not by a stream of benefits but by a stream of abuse. British Rail's advanced multiple units for the newly electrified Bedford–St Pancras ('Bed-Pan') line gathered much rust before manning levels were finally agreed. In theory, the estimates can make good financial sense. In practice, the people may be unwilling to conform to the script.

In opthalmology, 20/20 vision represents perfect sight. Raking through the ashes of burnt-out projects can produce a visual phenomenon unknown to science, 20/20 hindsight. In retrospect, how could eminently sensible people in the mid 1970s believe in a world full of randy Californian bachelors panting to buy John Z. De Lorean's gull-winged, stainless steel ego chariot? At the time it seemed to make sense and would confer inestimable benefits on Belfast. In retrospect, in the early 1960s, how could eminently sensible people believe in a world full of jet-setting businessmen agog for supersonic travel? At the time it made sense and would confer inestimable benefits on the British aviation industry. But when the dream has proved to be a nightmare, the queues form to throw dead cats at yesterday's visionaries. In 1869, the London stock-broking firm of Overend Gurney collapsed and the financial world, for a brief time, teetered on the brink of chaos. 'Even a child,' anathematized Walter Bagehot, 'could have seen through the stupidity of their investment policy.' Well, yes, but . . . more realistic are the words of an academic, financially drenched when the South Sea Bubble went 'pop' in 1721: 'When the rest of the world are mad, we must imitate in some measure.'

So what can possibly go wrong with the fourth variable, the estimated terminal value of the asset? In the eighteenth century,

Imperial Russia made an intermittent and desultory investment in 586,400 square miles of inhospitable terrain called 'Russian America' or Alaska. Until 1861, Alaska was controlled by a merchant company but in that year it was duly assimilated into the Russian Empire and an Imperial Governor appointed. The odd fur was trapped, the occasional whale harpooned, but the kopeks flowing in far from matched the roubles flowing out. Mother Russia decided to divest. A deal was struck with the US Secretary of State, Seward, and, in 1867, Alaska joined the Republic at a terminal value of $7.2m. In Washington D.C., Seward was criticized for his profligacy and the deal was branded 'Seward's Folly'. In 1896, gold was discovered in the Yukon, the gold rush was underway. In the next fifty years, $1bn of minerals were extracted from the 'Folly'. In the 1960s, significant deposits of oil were discovered. By 1984, Alaska, the 49th State of the Union, was producing 20 per cent of the crude oil consumed in the United States.

The problem with the fifth variable, the appropriate discount factor, is obvious. We assume interest rates are constant over time, more specifically over the life of the project. The interest rate (discount factor) selected is crucial in determining the worthwhileness of the project in terms of net present value and in terms of the differential between internal rate of return and the cost of capital. But a glance at the real world shows that interest rates do vary and vary substantially. In the UK, between 1975 and 1980, the base rate was as low as 8 per cent and as high as 16 per cent.

The five variables in the equation of worthwhileness – capital cost and completion time, useful asset life, annual cash flows, terminal value and discount factor – necessarily contain elements of uncertainty. Further, the five variables are not hermetically sealed boxes of specific uncertainty. Uncertainty is inherent in the interactions between the variables themselves and between the variables and the wider environment in which they operate.

In his book, *Great Planning Disasters*, Peter Hall identifies three categories of uncertainty:

(i) uncertainty in the relevant planning environment, that is, within the five variables themselves – cost overruns, time slippage, inaccurate assessments of demand, etc.

(ii) uncertainty about decisions in related areas – competitors, politicians, technological change, etc.

(iii) uncertainty about potential shifts in value judgements: changes in wider social attitudes may have an impact on the project –flight from the inner cities, antipathy to motorway development, suspicion of nuclear projects, etc.

Hall neatly points up the scope for interaction between the categories of uncertainty with reference to the Concorde project. In the relevant planning environment, uncertainty was inherent in the adaptation of existing technology (military supersonic aircraft) to a new purpose (civil aviation). This facet of uncertainty revealed itself in cost and time overruns. Annual cash flows, on the revenue side, were based on an assessment of the premium consumers would pay for quicker travel in comparison with conventional aircraft. Cost and time overruns added to this premium with a scaling down of demand and revenue. Meanwhile, in related decision areas the competition (Boeing, Lockheed, McDonnel Douglas) was modifying the nature of its product. The development of wide-bodied jets reduced both journey time and cost per seat mile. The basis of the premium, time saved, was eroded while the reduction in cost increased the premium further. The premium was increasing while the benefit was diminishing. In another related decision area, oil was no longer a cheap resource: its price was rising rapidly. In absolute terms, this increased the cost of air travel, but relatively, the impact was greater on those aircraft with low fuel-efficiency. Concorde, designed in an era of cheap oil, had the lowest fuel efficiency of all. The premium increased still further. Meanwhile societal value judgements were changing. The brave new technological world of the 1960s was replaced by a more environmentally sensitive era. One of these sensitivities was noise. Developments in conventional aircraft had produced a generation of quieter engines. Concorde was left with noisy take-off and landing characteristics. There was also the problem of the supersonic boom. As a result, operations were restricted to a narrow range of routes with a further reduction in demand and revenue. Instead of the estimated 400 sales, only nine Concordes were eventually sold.

We have examined earlier, and essayed answers to, the three fundamental questions of worthwhileness:

  (i) is it worthwhile to the firm to invest in the project?

 (ii) which among mutually exclusive routes to the same objective is it *more* worthwhile for the firm to adopt?

(iii) where resources are finite, which mix of projects is it *most* worthwhile for the firm to adopt?

Given the uncertainty attaching to estimates of the future, the hierarchy of worthwhileness questions can be seen to rely upon an even more fundamental question:

(iv) how robust are the estimates which are fed into the hierarchy, the ingredients in the logic process depicted at Figure 19?

A variety of techniques, based largely on probability theory, have been developed which are beyond the scope of this book. A more straightforward approach is through 'sensitivity analysis'.

Sensitivity analysis is designed to answer 'what if' questions. What if the capital cost is x per cent greater than estimated? What if completion time is x months longer than estimated? What if net cash is x per cent lower than estimated? The answer to such questions enables a view to be taken on how much cover the estimates contain against such eventualities.

Assume that we are dealing with a project to establish a production line, based on existing technology, to turn out an innovatory product. On the basis of experience with similar production lines inside and outside the firm, we estimate the capital cost at £8m and completion time at one year. Again, experience indicates that similar installations have a useful life of three years and a nil terminal value. Given that we are dealing with the world of the known, the uncertainty attaching to these estimates is relatively low. Uncertainty relates to estimates of annual cash flows, particularly revenues. We are marketing a new product. Market research indicates the following net cash flows:

	£m
Year 1	6.0
Year 2	5.0
Year 3	3.0

Our cost of capital is assessed at 10 per cent.

We can now insert the estimates into the worthwhileness machine in the normal manner:

	Cash Inflow/ (Outflow) £m	Discount Factor (10%)	Discounted Cash Flow £m
Initial outlay	(8.0)	—	(8.0)
Year 1	6.0	0.909	5.5
Year 2	5.0	0.826	4.1
Year 3	3.0	0.751	2.3
		Gross present value	11.9
	LESS	Initial outlay	(8.0)
		Net present value	3.9

If we continue the process we find, by trial and error, that the internal rate of return (that discount factor which produces an NPV of zero) is 40 per cent:

	Cash Inflow/ (Outflow) £m	Discount Factor (40%)	Discounted Cash Flow £m
Initial outlay	(8.0)	—	(8.0)
Year 1	6.0	0.714	4.3
Year 2	5.0	0.510	2.6
Year 3	3.0	0.364	1.1
		Gross present value	8.0
	LESS	Initial outlay	(8.0)
		Net present value	—

147

An IRR of 40 per cent, when compared with a cost of capital of 10 per cent, appears highly attractive. But how robust is the most vulnerable component, estimated annual cash flows? What if the net cash flows turned out to be 10 per cent less than estimated? Given the innovatory nature of the product, what if the shortfall were as high as 20 per cent? Indeed, how great a shortfall could be sustained without sending the IRR below the cost of capital? By recalculation, we find:

	Internal Rate of Return %
At estimated annual net cash flows	40
10% shortfall on estimate	31
20% shortfall on estimate	22
33% shortfall on estimate	10 (= cost of capital)

So, estimates of annual cash flows can stand a fall of 33 per cent and the project can still, given no capital cost or completion time overruns, meet the cost of capital. Is this a sufficient margin of safety? *Prima facie*, it is. But what does the accumulated experience, non-rational touch and feel of senior managers indicate? If these vibrations are also good, then the project should go ahead.

In some projects, uncertainty may reside in more than one variable in the equation of worthwhileness. This is often the case where both the technology and the market are new. In these cases, sensitivity analysis can be applied to a composite 'disaster scenario'. Assume our production line involved new technology. We might now probe not only the estimates of cash flows but also the estimates of capital cost and completion time. Uncertainty might be translated into a multiple 'what if' question. What if . . .

(i) capital cost exceeded estimate by 10 per cent?
(ii) completion slipped by one year?
(iii) annual cash flows were 20 per cent less than estimated?

The 'disaster scenario' can be evaluated:

	Cash Inflow/ (Outflow) £m	Discount Factor (10%)	Discounted Cash Flow £m
Year 0: *initial outlay*	(4.4)	—	(4.4)
Year 1: *initial outlay*	(4.4)	0.909	(4.0)
Year 2	4.8	0.826	4.0
Year 3	4.0	0.751	3.0
Year 4	2.4	0.683	1.6
		Gross present value	8.6
	LESS	Initial outlay	(8.4)
		Net present value	0.2

Even in the 'disaster scenario', the NPV is positive. Hence the IRR exceeds the cost of capital. The project appears to be proof against disaster.

It is possible to take account of the differential impact of uncertainty in establishing required rates of return for different categories of project. Where the project involves the use of mature technology to supply a mature market, a relatively small premium over cost of capital may be considered adequate. At the other extreme, new technology/new market, a substantial premium may be sought:

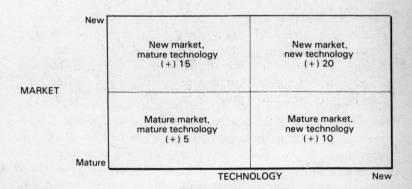

The figures indicate the premium required on the cost of capital. If the latter were 10 per cent, a project involving new markets and new technology would be required to achieve an IRR of 30 per cent. Additional premia may be applied when the investment is being undertaken abroad. An index of political stability can be constructed and weightings applied to the above required returns. If we assume a weighting of ($\times$)2 for the least politically stable countries, with a 10 per cent cost of capital, the required return for the least uncertain category (mature market/mature technology) would be 30 per cent. In this case, the surest way to turn an uncertain into a certain future is to have the index published. The return then becomes irrelevant. Your assets will be expropriated.

Payback techniques, properly understood, can be used to reinforce sensitivity analysis. Assume that two mutually exclusive projects each involve an initial outlay of £10k with similar installation time and asset life. Cash flows are estimated as follows:

	Project A £k	Project B £k
Initial outlay	10	10
Net cash inflows		
Year 1	6	1
Year 2	4	4
Year 3	2	5
Year 4	2	8
Year 5	2	8
PAYBACK	*2 years*	*3 years*

Project A 'pays back' its initial outlay one year sooner than Project B. It is important to realize that payback, as a means of assessing the worthwhileness of alternative projects, is heavily flawed. Apart from ignoring the time-value theory of money, it takes no account of income flows after the year in which payback is achieved. *Après le payback, la deluge* . . . As such, as a method of assessing worthwhileness, payback shares philosophical roots with the devotees of the Anglo-Israeli Sect. In 1938 the Sect predicted the end of the world in 1940. Early in 1941, after much deliberation, the Sect announced that the world had, in fact, ended but no one had noticed. Payback should not be used to evaluate worthwhileness. However, payback can be used as a indicator of uncertainty.

The further in the future the benefit is estimated to fall, the greater the uncertainty which attaches to it. The payback period represents the time for which the initial outlay is hung out. The shorter the payback, the greater the likelihood that the grubstake, at least, will be recouped. And, in some cases, there may be a genuine threat of wipe-out in the form of expropriation, law-suits, legislation, bankruptcy of major customer, etc. Payback, then, is an adjunct to, not a replacement for, DCF techniques of investment appraisal.

The appearance of the project, then, should not be confused with the reality. The reality is that the feedstock of investment appraisal techniques comprises not fact but estimate. Estimates inevitably contain elements of risk and uncertainty. Such characteristics are inherent in each of the variables in the equation of worthwhileness. Risk and uncertainty also reside in the interactions between the variables themselves and between the variables and the wider context in which they operate. The presence of risk and uncertainty is *not* a prescription for risk-aversive behaviour. Rather, it is a prescription for making the risk and the uncertainty explicit and for testing the robustness of the estimates on which the appraisal is based. Otherwise, the menu can easily be confused with the meal.

Just as the menu should not be confused with the meal, so a part of management should not be confused with the whole. When the subject of capital investment is approached from the direction of financial techniques, it is easy to succumb to the myth of the rational manager and to believe that the allocation of capital resources is entirely a matter of logic, reason and analysis. Similarly, over-emphasis on the financial techniques of appraisal can disguise the fact that appraisal is only one aspect of a wider content which contains three major components:

(i) identification of investment opportunities
(ii) analysis
(iii) implementation

If the analytical component is over-emphasized, even if the other two components are recognized, the whole content can easily be interpreted as entirely logical and analytical. Ideas are seen to emerge from a structured scanning of the environment, estimates are systematically calculated with due statistical allowance for uncertainty, worthwhileness is rationally evaluated by DCF techniques, decisions are determined by financial ranking, implementation is analytically programmed and scientifically monitored. But, just as appraisal is only one component of a wider content, so logic, reason and analysis are only part of a wider process.

Henry Mintzberg, in an article in 1976, examined perceptions of management in relation to the processes of the human brain. Research suggested that, in the left-hand hemisphere of the brain, the logical, analytical, intellectual functions were performed. The right-hand hemisphere was the locus for the less rational and programmable processes – intuition, imagination, vision, emotion. Mintzberg argued that many perceptions of management equated the process of management exclusively with the process of the left-hand hemisphere. However, experience and observation indicated that this was too restricted a view of management. The processes associated with the right-hand hemisphere – vision, creativity and flair – were also supremely important particularly in situations which involved a high level of ambiguity. 'Soft' information – hunch, guess, hearsay, impression – were just as influential as the 'hard' figures.

Mintzberg's musings have relevance to the three components of capital resource-allocation.

(a) Identification may be a purely rational process. An inefficient machine may cause pain in the productive system of the firm. Several replacements are readily identifiable.

DCF techniques isolate which is most worthwhile. Acquire, install, operate, *finis*. New market opportunities may emerge from a comprehensive scanning of the business environment. However, identification of new processes, new markets, new solutions to old problems, new combinations of existing variables, often involves an element of the non-rational. The intuitive complements the logical, the imaginative the analytical. The result is inspiration, 'the sudden cessation of ignorance'. 'What would the world look like,' asked the young Einstein, recumbent in a Swiss pasture, 'if I rode on a beam of light?' Part of the answer was the Theory of Relativity. The logic, reason and analysis to substantiate the theory came later. A chance event, a random combination of everyday occurrences, an unusual perspective on a commonplace phenomenon, a chord is struck in the organ-loft of the mind and the seedlings of a capital investment project are sown.

(b) Analysis, paradoxically, is not immune to non-rational, non-cerebral influences. As we have seen, estimates are the feedstock of analysis in capital investment appraisal and the analysis is made in the context of future time. We are dealing with uncertainty and ambiguity, commodities as difficult to pin down as a globule of mercury. In this context, no amount of statistical technique or sensitivity analysis can remove every trace of doubt. You may think it's the greatest idea since soft toilet paper, but you're not quite sure. In this situation, hunch, feel, 'nose' can be just as important as the outputs of the logic machine. And the visceral quality of courage will be required to back your hunch with the scarce resources of the firm.

(c) Implementation, too, can appear nicely rational and programmable: 'critical path analysis' (CPA), precise systems for monitoring and control, organizational skills and problem-solving techniques. But what happens when the sub-contractor goes bust, when the construction gang goes on strike, when Mother Nature moves a physical feature, like a river, just enough to foul up the plans? Often the answer lies not in the left-hand hemisphere of the brain but in the right – imagination, intuition, emotion. And sometimes the answer lies not in the mind but in the guts – battlefield valour, animal cunning.

The identification, analysis and implementation of a successful capital investment project takes in the whole panoply of managerial skills, knowledge and attitudes. Logic, reason and analysis are necessary but not sufficient for success. To ignore this is to confuse a part of the process with the whole. And such a confusion can lead to a state of corporate constipation known as 'analysis paralysis'.

Major capital investment decisions determine the future shape of the firm. And the decisions, once made, are often irreversible. If the decision turns up trumps, the image is that of Sir Christopher Wren, '*si monumentum requiras, circumspice*' – portrait on boardroom wall, name on ubiquitous plaques, eponymous Head Office. But can the success be repeated? St Paul's Cathedral is a hard act to follow. Remember the sage of *The Hitchhiker's Guide to the Galaxy*, Slartybardfast. Slarty was a designer of coastlines: Norway, with its myriad coastal indentations, was his masterpiece. But his design for Africa lay rejected – too many fjords. If the decision turns into a lead balloon, then listen to the Shah of Persia in exile: 'When things go wrong, everything is a mistake.' When a major capital investment goes wrong, the processes of Greek tragedy take over: 'Hubris', the defiance of the Gods, the overweening arrogance which confused the menu with the meal; 'Ate', the anger of the Gods visited on a market totally underwhelmed by the product. Soothsayers are now in full sooth – the City whispering, the banks muttering, the creditors fidgetting. In the business schools scripts are being re-written – a case study in enrepreneurial excellence becomes a study in corporate collapse. Enter stage left 'Nemesis', divine retribution, opprobrium, obloquy, Carey St, taken over for a song. Life is an unmade bed.

Major capital investment projects are the soap operas of the financial world.

9. Getting It All Together

'. . . The only really successful managers I have met manage to do both – to keep an eye on the big things that count while paying meticulous attention to the little things that count as well.'

Alistair Mant: The Rise and Fall of the British Manager

One hundred miles above the surface of the Earth, a military reconnaissance satellite (a 'spy in the sky') quietly manoeuvres itself into place. Its beady electronic eye is designed to scan the enemy's backyard, the parts conventional fieldcraft does not reach. The power of its eyesight is formidable. NASA's space telescope, planned for launch in 1986, has the capacity to pick up details of the Galilean satellites of Jupiter, 400 million miles distant from Earth. Turn this capacity back on to the surface of the Earth and no amount of back-combing will disguise the smallest of bald spots from the gremlin in the Kremlin or the Spooks of Foggy Bottom. But such capacity carries with it a problem. The closer you look, the more you see. The more detailed the examination, the greater the reassurance that nothing has been missed. But the closer the look, the greater the difficulty in shaping and patterning the multiplicity of phenomena bombarding the sensory equipment. The latest series of Landsat satellites can transmit 118 million bits of information per second. Look too close and the system risks information overload and 'data pollution'.

We are faced with the same problem in attempting to monitor the state of the financial territory. At the one extreme we have the Nitty Grittialist School: nuts and bolts, amps and volts: 'hands on' with a proclivity for digging up the plant to vouchsafe that the roots are healthy. 'No surprises' is the aim. At the other extreme we have the Laid Back Tendency: broad perspectives, helicopter minds, provide the right soil, nutriment and climate and let a thousand flowers bloom.

Anthony Sampson's account of International Telephone and Telegraph (ITT) under Harold S. Geneen portrays a system in pursuit of the unshakeable facts. Large, formal meetings of senior managers with accountable official in attendance; a mighty avoirdupois of statistical information; an overhead projector, a screen of cinemascope proportions, slide after slide of tabulated figures, each one picked out by the arrow-head of a light-pen. Responsible official called to account each time the arrow-head stopped.

Lord Weinstock and GEC project an entirely different image. Small head office, no corporate planning department, much operational autonomy, encouragement of diversity but tight as well as loose – close involvement in budgetting, monthly monitoring of thirty performance indicators and seven key ratios.

In getting the act together, then, we need to design a reconnaissance system which will detect, at an early state, major developments in the financial territory but which will avoid data pollution. We need to scan the main features of the financial territory on a continuous basis. We also require an auxiliary function. Whenever we detect some change in one of the main features, we need the capability to zoom in and examine in minute detail the foothills as well as the mountains, the villages as well as the towns, the bridle-paths as well as the motorways. If the need arises, we require the capability to read the number-plates of the car parked outside 39 Acacia Avenue, Dnepropetrovsk.

What, then, are the main features of the financial territory which require continuous scanning? They are three in number:

  (i) financial performance
 (ii) solvency
(iii) liquidity

Ratios provide the main monitoring mechanism. The three features are examined in turn.

1. Financial performance

A pyramid of ratios can be erected to monitor financial performance. At the apex of the pyramid is the indicator 'return on investment' (ROI) or, 'return on capital employed' (ROCE). This indicator is the ratio of:

$$\frac{\text{profit before interest and tax}}{\text{capital employed}}$$

The ratio is expressed as a percentage. By using profit before interest, distortions caused by differing leverage factors are avoided. Similarly, by taking profit before tax, the idiosyncracies of the company's tax position are kept well away from this indicator of performance. As we have seen, because of the dual concept, capital employed equates to net assets:

$$\text{shareholders' funds } (+) \text{ loan capital} =$$
$$\text{fixed assets } (+) \text{ working capital}$$

ROI, the prime performance indicator, is, in turn, determined by two other ratios, profit margin and asset turnover. Profit margin is the ratio:

$$\frac{\text{profit before interest and tax}}{\text{sales}}$$

expressed as a percentage. Asset turnover is the ratio:

$$\frac{\text{sales}}{\text{net assets}}$$

Asset turnover shows how many £s of sales are generated by £1 of assets. The relationship can be expressed as follows:

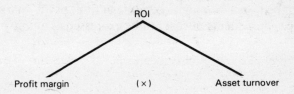

157

Assume the following data in the Published Accounts of a company:

		£m
(a)	Sales	100
(b)	Profit before interest and tax	5
(c)	Capital employed/net assets	25

ROI is 20 per cent (b/c). The determinants are a profit margin of 5 per cent (b/a) and an asset turnover of four (a/c):

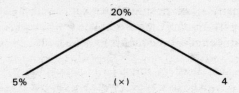

In brief, the prime indicator (ROI) is dependent not only on profit margin but also on the efficiency and effectiveness with which the fixed assets and working capital of the firm are utilized (asset turnover). It follows that, if improvement in ROI is sought or reasons for deterioration are required, both dimensions, profitability and asset utilization, must be scanned.

First, examine the dimension of profitability. A ratio, by definition, expresses in a single number a comparison between two numbers. In the case of profit margin, the two numbers are profit (before interest and tax) and sales. As we have seen, profit is the difference between sales and the cost of these sales. Costs, then, are a major determinant of profit margin. The different components of cost can be expressed as a ratio of sales:

Further sub-divisions are possible within each cost item. Overhead, for example, can be sub-analyzed into its constituent parts and ratios such as R & D/sales and head office expenses/sales derived. Sales and profit can be related not only to the cost of resources but also to the number of resources utilized. Sales per employee and profit per employee can be used as indicators of labour productivity. Sales, too, can be analyzed in isolation from costs. If the firm is pursuing a policy of diversification and product innovation, progress can be measured by the ratio:

$$\frac{\text{sales of product introduced in last 3 years}}{\text{total sales}}$$

If the objective is geographical diversification away from the UK, performance can be monitored by use of the ratio:

$$\frac{\text{non-UK sales}}{\text{total sales}}$$

Obviously, profitability increases stem from higher sales or lower costs or both. Subsidiary ratios provide the means for monitoring and analyzing progress.

In addition to profitability, we need to scan the determinants of asset turnover. If more sales can be generated from the same net assets, then, with profit margin unchanged, ROI will increase. In our example, if asset turnover could be increased from 4 to 5, with a profit margin steady at 5 per cent, ROI would increase from 20 per cent to 25 per cent. As with profit margin, asset turnover can be disaggregated into its major causal components and subsidiary ratios can be derived:

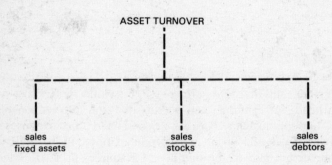

The ratio sales/fixed assets needs to be treated with caution when comparisons over time are being made. As we have seen, fixed assets are written down each year in the amount of the annual depreciation charge. The reduction in asset value is rarely matched by a reduction in sales generated. Accordingly, an improvement in the ratio over time can result solely from the senescence of fixed assets. In addition, if assets have recently been leased which previously were owned, in comparison with previous periods the fixed asset valuation will be reduced and the ratio increased. In this case, there could be an offsetting reduction in profit margin if the leasing charge exceeded the annual depreciation charge of the owned asset. Again, the ratio can be subdivided into different categories of fixed assets and supported by indicators of asset utilization such as:

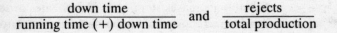

$$\frac{\text{down time}}{\text{running time } (+) \text{ down time}} \quad \text{and} \quad \frac{\text{rejects}}{\text{total production}}$$

The second determinant of asset turnover,

$$\frac{\text{sales}}{\text{stocks}}$$

or 'stock turnover' can be disaggregated into its component parts:

Again, caveats need to be entered in the use of these ratios. Ideally, the numerator and denominator of a ratio should be expressed in the same value terms. In stock ratios the numerator (sales) includes an element of profit which is omitted from stock valuations. Comparisons between companies can be distorted if different bases (LIFO, FIFO, see Chapter 3) are used for stock valuation. Finally, stocks can be subject to fluctuation because of seasonal factors. The year-end figure shown in the published balance sheet of the company is not necessarily representative.

The third determinant of asset turnover, sales/debtors, is usually converted into the firm's 'average collection period' and expressed in days. If annual sales are £25m and average debtors £5m, debtor turnover is five. If the debtor turnover is divided into 365 days, the result (73 days) is the average period taken by the firm to collect its debts. Obviously, a reduction in the collection period will increase asset turnover.

The key indicator of financial performance, return on investment, and its two determinants, profit margin and asset turnover, can be continuously monitored. Where change takes place or improvement is sought, subsidiary determinants can also be isolated.

Moving from the general to the particular, a hierarchy of performance ratios can be assembled (Figure 20). The ratios derived can be compared with past trends, budgets and competing companies.

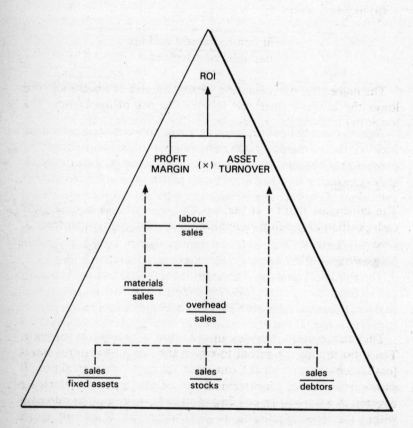

Figure 20: *Pyramid of ratios*

2. Solvency

We have already met the major indicators of solvency in Chapter 6. They are:
  (a) debt ratio:

$$\frac{\text{long-term loans}}{\text{long-term loans} + \text{shareholders' funds}}$$

  (b) interest cover:

$$\frac{\text{profit before interest and tax}}{\text{loan interest payments}}$$

The higher the debt ratio, the greater the risk of insolvency. The lower the interest cover, the greater the risk of insolvency. The lower the interest cover, the greater the risk of default.

3. Liquidity

The third main feature in the territory of finance is liquidity, the cash position of the firm in relation to its maturing commitments. Two ratios are used:
  (a) current ratio:

$$\frac{\text{current assets}}{\text{current liabilities}}$$

The current ratio provides an indicator of short-term solvency. The ratio reveals the extent to which the firm's short-term assets (cash, debtors, and stock) can meet its short-term liabilities. It shows how far the short-term claims of the firm's creditors are covered by assets which can be expected to be converted into cash within the same time-scale as the claims. So, if current assets amounted to £10m and current liabilities to £5m, the current ratio would be two. In this case, the firm could liquidate its current assets at a discount of 50 per cent and still have the wherewithal to pay off its creditors in full.

(b) 'acid test' or 'quick ratio':

$$\frac{\text{liquid assets (current assets } (-) \text{ stocks)}}{\text{current liabilities}}$$

The current ratio is usually supplemented by the 'acid test'. The pertinence of the 'acid test' lies in its recognition that stocks are usually the least liquid component of current assets and are the item most likely to be sold at a heavy discount in a liquidation. In this context, an 'acid test' in excess of one indicates that, if the firm can collect from its debtors, creditors can be satisfied without the liquidation of stocks.

It is possible, then, through ratio analysis, to establish a reconnaissance system which monitors on a continuous basis the three main features of the financial territory. The system also has the capability, when required, to home in on the main features and expose contributory detail. The schema of the system in terms of the main features (performance, solvency and liquidity) is shown at Figure 21.

1. PERFORMANCE

(a) Return on investment (ROI): $\dfrac{\text{profit before interest and tax}}{\text{capital employed}}$ %

(b) Profit margin: $\dfrac{\text{profit before interest and tax}}{\text{sales}}$ %

(c) Asset turnover: $\dfrac{\text{sales}}{\text{net assets}}$ (times)

(d) Fixed asset turnover: $\dfrac{\text{sales}}{\text{fixed assets}}$ (times)

(e) Stock turnover: $\dfrac{\text{sales}}{\text{stocks}}$ (times)

(f) Debtor turnover: $\dfrac{\text{sales}}{\text{debtors}}$ (times)

2. SOLVENCY

(a) Debt ratio: $\dfrac{\text{long-term loans}}{\text{long-term loans} (+) \text{shareholders' funds}}$ %

(b) Interest cover: $\dfrac{\text{profit before interest and tax}}{\text{interest payments on loans}}$ (times)

3. LIQUIDITY

(a) Current ratio: $\dfrac{\text{current assets}}{\text{current liabilities}}$ (times)

(b) Acid test: $\dfrac{\text{current assets} (-) \text{stocks}}{\text{current liabilities}}$ (times)

Figure 21: Ratio analysis

The schema, then, can be used for internal monitoring against past trends and budgets. It can also be used in financial detective work on the published accounts of other companies. Consider the following data extracted from the Published Accounts of a British company over a three-year period:

	Year 1 £m		Year 2 £m		Year 3 £m	
Turnover	19.3		21.2		16.7	
Profit before taxation	5.6		3.0		(1.2)	
	£m	£m	£m	£m	£m	£m
Current assets:						
stocks	2.1		3.3		3.1	
debtors	3.4		4.7		5.0	
cash, bank, short-term deposits	2.5		0.4		0.2	
	——	8.0	——	8.4	——	8.3
Current liabilities:						
creditors	(1.5)		(1.9)		(2.2)	
overdraft	(0.2)		(1.6)		(2.8)	
taxation	(3.0)		(2.2)		—	
dividend	(0.1)	(4.8)	(0.1)	(5.8)	—	(5.0)
Net current assets		3.2		2.6		3.3
Fixed assets		5.0		6.8		7.0
Net assets		8.2		9.4		10.3
Shareholders' funds:						
share capital	1.9		2.2		2.2	
reserves	6.3		7.2		6.6	
		8.2		9.4		8.8
Loan capital		—		—		1.5
Capital employed		8.2		9.4		10.3

In an attempt to make sense out of this diverse financial phenomena, we follow the schema and construct our data base:

1. PERFORMANCE

		Year 1	Year 2	Year 3
(a) Return on investment	(%)	68	32	(12)
(b) Profit margin	(%)	29	14	(7)
(c) Asset turnover	(times)	2.3	2.2	1.6
(d) Fixed asset turnover	(times)	3.9	3.1	2.4
(e) Stock turnover	(times)	9.2	6.4	5.4
(f) Debtor turnover	(times)	5.7	4.5	3.3
(Average collection period (days))		64	81	111

2. SOLVENCY

(a) Debt ratio	(%)	—	—	14.6
(b) Interest cover				N/A

3. LIQUIDITY

(a) Current ratio	(times)	1.7	1.4	1.7
(b) Acid test	(times)	1.2	0.9	1.0

Notes: interest payments are not separately divulged; hence 'profit before taxation' is used in the appropriate ratios. Similiarly, 'cost of sales' is not separately available for use in stock turnover. Year-end figures, rather than the average of opening and closing balances, are used.

The vertiginous decline in the prime performance indicator, ROI, suggests that our firm has experienced a not uneventful three years. But did it jump or was it pushed? Was it simply the hapless victim of circumstances or were the injuries self-inflicted? In seeking answers, we need to sift the central from the peripheral and to separate cause from effect. A knowledge of detective fiction is useful. The art of the English detective story lies in constructing a relatively uncomplicated and logical set of circumstances and then allowing this simple plot to marinate in a rich sauce of concealment, evasion and obfuscation. Around a straightforward sequence of cause and effect, an elaborate puzzle is fashioned. How has the intruder entered the locked room? What was the strange smell on the landing? Why is the Mother Superior wearing high-heeled shoes? To discover whodunnit, we need to isolate the basic plot, identify the pattern of causation and ignore the exotica. 'Eliminate the impossible,' says Sherlock Holmes, 'and what remains, however improbable, is the truth.' And, if all else fails, blame the evaporating ice dart which has done the damage and disappeared without trace.

So, a cursory inspection of ROI suggests that there has been dirty work at the crossroads. But, as we have seen, ROI is an effect not a cause. Causation is shown in the relationship:

$$ROI = profit\ margin\ (\times)\ asset\ turnover$$

In Year 1 the relationship produced sweet music. For every £1 of sales, 29p was profit while every £1 tied up in net assets generated £2.30 of sales. ROI has reached a Himalayan peak of 68 per cent and, in financial terms, we are eating caviar off the finest china to the accompaniment of heavenly choirs. But is the air too rarefied to sustain activity? In Year 2, ROI is reduced to 32 per cent. Now, in the broad sweep of things, this is to reduce the return from Himalayan to Alpine proportions, from the miraculous to the merely magical. After all, profitability of 14 per cent and asset turnover of 2.2 ain't exactly hay. But the significant fact is that the ROI in Year 2 is over 50 per cent less than the ROI in Year 1. We have a suspicious circumstance. Is all what it appears to be?

Logically, ROI has declined in Year 2 because both profit margin and asset turnover have fallen. The factors which determine profit margin are selling price and cost per unit. As we have seen, if there is a significant proportion of fixed costs in the cost structure, volume can also be an important influence. Introduce a spot of hypothesis. If volume is not increasing but, through inflation, costs are, then margin will reduce. In addition, to stimulate increased volume, price may be reduced and margin will be further reduced. Turnover in Year 2 has increased but not much above the rate of inflation. Now hypothesize further. If this relatively static volume has occurred when expansion was planned, when fixed costs (depreciation, advertising, distribution) were increased in anticipation of greater volume, then margins will be further eroded. Pursue this hypothesis in respect of asset turnover.

Although sales have increased by 10 per cent, asset turnover in Year 2 has declined. Fixed asset turnover has declined by nearly 20 per cent. Fixed assets themselves have increased by 36 per cent (£5m to £6.8m). This would indicate that expansion was indeed planned. Further, the increase in stocks (2.1m to 3.3.m) and consequent decline in stock turnover suggests that the additional fixed assets were utilized but the end product was not expanded sales but increased stocks. And, in an attempt to move these stocks, credit periods were extended from an average of 64 to 81 days with a consequential reduction in debtor turnover from 5.7 to 4.5.

But solvency does not appear, at this stage, to be threatened. There is no long-term debt but a small cloud, no bigger than a man's hand, has appeared in the form of an overdraft and 'cash bank and short-term deposits' show signs of evaporation. In terms of liquidity, current assets could be disposed of at a discount of 30 per cent and current liabilities met (current ratio 1.4) but, in the acid test, debtors and cash balances alone would not meet current liabilities in full.

We have reached the stage in the detective novel when the scene has been set, the characters introduced and an air of expectancy created. In the English country house, night has fallen, and the butler has locked the doors and turned out the lights. The guests have retired. All is quiet. And then . . . the screams start, lights come on and the bodies begin to pile up. We have reached Year 3.

Year 3 represents the *dénouement* of the causative factors already identified. Volume and profit margin collapse but fixed assets continue to increase. Production outstrips demand and stocks pile up. In an attempt to move product, average collection period increases still further.

In terms of solvency, debt has to be introduced with a leverage of 14.6 per cent. Overdraft also increases. Liquidity, in the form of the current ratio, appears to improve but pressure has been taken off current liabilities by the introduction of long-term debt. If debtors pay up, current liabilities could be settled, but debtors are taking an increasingly long time to do so.

The plot, then, is relatively simple. A company is enjoying a period of huge success. This success is reflected in an ROI of 68 per cent. Profit margins are enormous and asset turnover is brisk. Fired by this success, the company adopts a policy of expansion: fixed assets are increased and fixed costs are incurred. But just when the wherewithal of expansion is complete, the market, far from increasing, takes a nose-dive. The company is left with over-capacity and fixed costs to be absorbed by a declining volume of sales. Sales fall faster than production. Margins decline, fixed assets are under-utilized, stocks build up and credit periods are elongated. Long-term debt is introduced to fund the increased amount of cash trapped in the firm.

Who dunnit? What caused sales volume to decline? All the suspects file into the Library of the country house where the great detective awaits. This is the bit where, with much use of flashbacks, the central is sifted from the peripheral, cause is distinguished from effect and, to gasps of astonishment and much swooning, the assassin is unmasked. When we are assembled, Poirot takes us through the plot, explains the decline in ROI, expatiates on the acid test and then answers the question we are all asking. Who dunnit? He whips a green baize cloth off an antique table to reveal the villain of the piece – a die-cast model car with friction-free wheels made by a US toy manufacturer. For the firm we have been investigating was Lesney Products, makers of Matchbox Toys, the industrial shooting star of the 1960s. Between 1963 and 1969 (Year 1 in our schema), pre-tax profits increased by a factor of ten and market growth, world-wide, seemed limitless. Then the competition introduced 'hotwheels', cars with friction-free wheels which, with a minimum of propulsion, would run and perform amazing feats on inexpensive tracks. And pimply school-boys throughout the world switched their preferences and their pocket money to the new technology with never a thought for the impact on ROI. The unimproved Matchbox toy became a collector's item.

In his autobiography, John Mortimer tells of his barrister father's greatest case, wherein he proved adultery on a single piece of evidence – an inverted footprint on the dash-board of an Austin 7. Ratio analysis takes a more mundane approach to cause and effect. The major features – performance, solvency and liquidity – are scanned. When one of these indicators shows signs of suspicious behaviour, ratio analysis provides the capability to zoom in for a close look at the contributory indicators. The pyramid of ratios provides a scanning mechanism for the financial territory and starts to pull the whole financial act together.

10. The Dyspepsia of Change

'We're all in favour of progress just so long as it doesn't involve change.'

Anon

The territory of finance is a deeply traditional land, close to its past and suspicious of change. The value system of the territory is enshrined in the syntax of its specialized language, in its concepts and conventions. Neatness and symmetry are highly esteemed: in the concept of the dual aspect there is a place for everything and everything is in its place; for every debit there is a credit. This is a tidy land: no litter, and dogs kept firmly on their leads. It is also a land in which the concrete is preferred to the abstract, practice rated higher than theory. Concepts like money measurement, going concern and historical cost limit the meaning of the language to the hard facts of corporate revenues and expenses, invoices, wage slips and bank statements. The language has difficulty in expressing concepts like human satisfactions, societal implications and other 'externalities' except insofar as they can be translated into corporate revenues and expenses. 'Creative accounting' is a pejorative term. It is a language suited to prose not poetry. The dominant architectural style is Classical rather than Romantic, good clean lines without a hint of curlicue or gargoyle.

The inhabitants of this land are uncomfortable with risk: the accrual and realization concepts enable a wary eye to be kept on commitment and obligations. The future is viewed with caution. Tomorrow will not necessarily be better than today. The convention of conservatism could be preached from a Calvinist pulpit: 'Face up to future losses now but do not take credit for future profits until they actually materialize.' Oscar Wilde would have been deeply unhappy in this land. For here no eighty-year-old man takes a twenty-year-old bride. Here it is experience which triumphs over hope. And, as in all traditional lands, it is important to maintain continuity with the past. In the words of the convention of consistency, 'all events of the same character are treated in the same fashion from one period to another'.

> 'Far from the madding crowd's ignoble strife
> Their sober wishes never learn'd to stray:
> Along the cool sequestered vale of life
> They kept the noiseless tenor of their way.'

W. C. Fields, comedian and student of human nature, conceived a deep hatred for Philadelphia. It represented in his mind all that was mean-spirited, dull and boring. Asked whether he had ever visited the City of Brotherly Love, he replied, 'Yes,' but it was closed.' As Fields, who never drank anything stronger than gin before breakfast, lay dying in a hospital bed, a young inexperienced priest happened upon him. He launched into a long description of the Kingdom of Heaven and concluded with a question: 'Are you not,' asked the novice, 'looking forward to joining your Maker in Heaven?' Fields pondered. 'On the whole,' he drawled, 'I'd rather be in Philadelphia.' To many non-accountants, the territory of finance is the Fieldsian Philadelphia writ large.

But value-systems do not spring into existence fully formed, they are not fashioned by nature. They emerge, adapt and are consolidated to serve a purpose. The territory of finance is inhabited by people who pursue a profession. The purpose of this profession is to produce sense and meaning out of diverse financial phenomena and to give assurance that such sense and meaning is both true and fair. To be able to make such pronouncements with credibility requires such qualities as integrity, impartiality and objectivity. These qualities in their turn rest on concepts like neatness, practicality, caution, rules and procedures. Soundness and a touch of gravitas are the keynotes. How much faith would you place in legal advice tendered by a solicitor who sported an eye-patch, an earring and a parrot on his shoulder? Would you trust medical advice proffered by a doctor with a safety-pin in his nose and bovver boots on his feet? Appropriate performance of the role is closely linked with the task the professional has to carry out. The value-system of the territory of finance is designed to produce people who can derive meaning from complex phenomena and can, with credibility, declare that this meaning represents a true and fair view of such phenomena.

But value-systems which esteem order and stability, by definition, have difficulty in coping with change. When confronted with change, the first reaction is usually defensive. The existence of change is accepted but the assumption is made that the change can be accommodated without disruption to the existing system. This is not necessarily retreatism, a drawing of the wagon train into a circle to fight off the Apaches of Innovation. It is rather a measure of confidence in the universality of the principles on which the system is based. There is also a tendency to see these principles as natural laws, universally applicable at all times and in all cases; change is transient but equations are for ever. But when experience shows that the system *is* feeling genuine pain, change can occur. The process, however, is evolutionary rather than revolutionary. It is tentative, feeling its way as it goes. As much of the old as possible is preserved. The very minimum of the new is admitted to achieve accommodation. The process of change in the territory of finance is like Walter Bagehot's mediaeval shirt: 'The executive must be like a shirt in the Middle Ages – extremely hard and extremely flexible: it must give way to attractive novelties which do not hurt; it must resist such as are dangerous; it must maintain old things which are good and fitting; it must alter such as cramp and give pain.' (The English Constitution.)

Two issues have recently cramped and pained the inhabitants of the territory of finance. The first is the phenomenon of persistently high levels of inflation. The second concerns the social role of the firm and involves menopausal considerations about the meaning of life. Is profit an end in itself? Can 'externalities' still be ignored in the advanced societies of the late twentieth century? Should the aim be, in Ruskin's words, 'not higher fortune but deeper felicity'? First, the specific issue of inflation. Then the more general issue of 'social accounting'.

Until the end of the 1960s, high levels of inflation were, in the UK, associated with other times and other places. In Europe, the Emperor Diocletian had, as early as the fourth century AD, attempted to deal with the ravages of inflation through his Edict on Prices. More recently the German inflation of 1923 was held up as an awful example. After the re-occupation of the Ruhr by French troops, the value of the mark against the dollar began to fall like a stone. On 1 July 1923, the mark stood at 160,000 to the dollar; on 1 August 1923, the mark touched 1 million to the dollar; by 1 November 1923, 130 million marks purchased a single dollar. And the more perceptive saw beyond the arithmetical progression to the political implications. The inflation destroyed faith in property and the meaning of money. Money ceased to be a medium of exchange and a store of value. '. . . the result of the inflation was to undermine the foundations of German society in a way which neither the war, nor the revolution of November 1918, nor the Treaty of Versailles had ever done.' More recently, in the UK, the phenomenon was associated with Latin American countries and was seen, like fences around football pitches, to be in some way connected with neo-Hispanic culture.

For, in the UK, before 1945 there was little experience either of high levels of inflation or of inflation as a persistent phenomenon. Between the end of the thirteenth century and the early Tudors, there appears to have been little change in the purchasing power of the currency. The sixteenth century did offer an example of persistent inflation at relatively high rates as the Old World economies assimilated the effect of New World gold: in that century, prices rose by a factor of five. But, between the Restoration and the start of the First World War, calm was restored and, apart from short-term dislocations, there was little change in the purchasing power of money. In the First World War price levels more than doubled but, in the inter-war years with recession and depression, there were periods when price levels fell rather than rose.

It was not until the end of the Second World War that persistent inflation returned to the UK. For the next twenty-five years, inflation was persistent but the rate was not high. Between 1945 and 1969, the Retail Price Index (RPI) increased at an average rate of 3 per cent per annum. Academics speculated on causation ('demand-pull' or 'cost-push'); governments took purchasing power out of the economy when the rate of increase accelerated ('stop-go'); but, by and large, the phenomenon was seen to provide a mild stimulus to business and to be a symptom of good times.

In the 1970s, perceptions and the phenomenon changed, Inflation persisted but it persisted at historically high levels:

Annual % Change in Retail Price Index

1970	1971	1972	1973	1974	1975	1976	1977	1978	1979	1980
6	9	7	9	16	24	16	16	8	13	13

Between 1975 and 1980, price levels doubled. Inflation was no longer associated with growth, unemployment escalated and times seemed less good.

How did all this affect the territory of finance? Under the money measurement concept, 'accounting records show only facts which can be expressed in monetary terms'. But persistently high rates of inflation were undermining the notion of money as a store of value which was uniform over time. As the above table shows, the Retail Price Index increased by 24% per cent in 1975: £1 of retained profit at the start of the year commanded considerably greater purchasing power than an equivalent sum at the end of the year. Companies could blandly announce that, in monetary terms, profits had increased. But, in an era of diminishing purchasing power, were these increases real or illusory? Did increased profits betoken growth or, when inflation was taken into account, did they disguise decline in real terms? Accounts based on traditional concepts and conventions could not provide an answer . . .

ACT 1, Scene 1

A flock of nimble-footed entrepreneurs are pondering opportunities for profitable investment in the entertainment sector. It is brought to their attention that a little-known musical ensemble, Biological Stains, is to represent Queen and Country in the forthcoming Eurovision Song Contest with a rendition of their latest opus, 'Mucus'. This, the entrepreneurs decide, will be a pangalactic megabiggy, particularly in the currently fashionable ear, nose and throat market. They promptly set up a company, Piratical Products Ltd, and invest in it £20k in the form of equity capital. They place with Sweat Shops PLC an order for twenty thousand T-shirts emblazoned with a portrait of the afore-mentioned virtuosi. The purchase price is £1 per vestment. The consignment is duly delivered, at the back door and after dark, and the transaction is swiftly completed in used notes of mixed denominations. Our entrepreneurs pause to check that their balance sheet balances:

	£k		£k
Share capital	20	Stocks	20

Reassured, they survey the stocked shirts and await the day of the contest. The mother-lode is only days away.

Scene 2

The contest is over. The entrepreneurs sit around a TV set with faces as long as fiddles. A bad trip! The Stains share last place with a warbling goatherd from Andorra. The mother-lode has turned into fool's gold. The T-shirts remain unsold, potentially unsale-able. The entrepreneurs speculate that they have made business history – the first firm to lose money by underestimating the public's taste. Disaster looms and the financial year rolls on.

Scene 3

A fortnight before the year-end and the Stains are back with a burp. In a single week they have grabbed four distinct segments of the market, A professor of structuralism has hailed 'Mucus' as a dithyrambic masterpiece, a tone poem evoking the lyricism of Sappho; the egg-heads come aboard. The lead guitarist has been busted on a coke-sniffing rap; the acid-heads join ship. The drummer has come out of the closet: gender-benders swarm up the gangplank. And Cretine, the troubadours' lead singer, has been photographed *tête-à-tête* with a Prince of the Blood Royal:

romantics everywhere book passage. The stocked raiment begins to sell like a new issue of Telecom shares. Just before the end of the financial year, the stock room is empty, the gear all sold at £1.25 per tog; £25k has found its way into the company's breadbin. The entrepreneurs link arms and sing 'There's no business like show business.'

INTERVAL

ACT 2, Scene 1

The financial year is over. The entrepreneurs come together for a board meeting. In attendance is Piratical Products' accountant. There are two items on the agenda: financial results for the year just ended and a discussion on future policy. Under Item 1 the accountant is invited to speak. 'Profit,' he flutes, 'is struck after comparing revenues and expenses, properly matched, over a finite period of time. Under the realization concept, revenue is recognized in the accounting period in which it is realized, that is during the accounting period in which the goods are actually dispatched to the customer. On this basis Piratical Products' sales revenue is £25k. Coincidentally, since all your sales were for cash, this amount in its entirety has flowed into the firm and resides in your bank account. To determine profit we need to match against this sales revenue the expenses incurred in achieving such a level of sales. The historical cost of the articles sold was £20k and you have no other expenses. Therefore you have made an operating or trading profit of £5k. Of this you will pay £2½k in corporation tax, leaving you £2½k available for distribution to shareholders. You must decide how much to distribute and how much to retain within the company. You have achieved a return on capital employed of 25 per cent, an impressive result in your first year in operation. I leave with you a copy of your Accounts duly certified as a true and fair record. Incidentally, my friend is a Stains fan. Could you get me their autograph?' (Exit Accountant.) The entrepreneurs defer a decision on distribution until after the discussion on future policy.

The company, they reason, has been a nice little earner. Demand for the clobber will hold up. After all, the Stains are about to release their follow-up to 'Mucus', an oratorio entitled 'Rheum With a View'. But best not to get too greedy. Keep the operation at the same level of sales and since no expansion is envisaged, the £2½k can be distributed in its entirety and trousered pronto. Pop a cheque in the post to the taxman for £2½k and future policy is simple – give Sweat Shops a bell and order twenty thousand of same.

ACT 2, Scene 2

A week later. Another board meeting. Two items on the agenda, a letter from Sweat Shops and the company's newly arrived bank statement. The letter is read out. 'Since your last order, the RPI (rag-trade price index) has increased by 10 per cent. Accordingly, the price of the merchandise has increased to £1.10 per article. Leave the back door open next Thursday night and twenty thousand bespoke singlets will steal into your stockrooms for a consideration of £22,000 in folding. And don't tell the VAT-man unless you want a fat lip.'

The bank statement is now considered. It shows:

Paradiso Bank, PO Box 26, Coral Island

	Credit	Debit	Balance
	£k	£k	£k
Initial capital	20	—	20
Purchase of T-shirts	—	20	—
Sales revenue	25	—	25
Taxation	—	2½	22½
Dividend	—	2½	20

How can this be? They have achieved an impressive profit and do not wish to expand. But there is insufficient cash in the business to maintain current levels of operation. They are saved from further puzzlement by the re-entry of the accountant in search of a photograph of the Stains' drummer. He appraises the situation and speaks.

'Your assessment is correct. Despite your profit and your desire not to expand existing operating capacity, there is insufficient cash in the business. Indeed, simply to maintain the status quo and replenish stock to its original levels will require an infusion of £2k into the business. The alternative is to scale down your operations and use your £20k to purchase 18,180 articles at the new price. The P & L Account, based as it was on historical cost principles, failed to disclose the impact of inflation. Of your £5k operating profits, £2k was, in a sense, an illusory surplus and needed to be retained in the business simply to offset the impact of inflation. Historical cost accounting is not designed to reflect this state of affairs, and the Inland Revenue chooses not to notice. But don't blame me. Rules are rules and in strict accordance with these rules your results represented a true and fair view of financial performance and position.'

(*Entrepreneurs start to yawn.*)

'Console yourselves further that the impact of inflation on your company is limited to the valuation of stocks. I have just conferred with the Board of Sweat Shops. They, as you know, have fixed as well as current assets. They installed a knitwear machine five years ago at a cost of £100k. They anticipated a useful life of five years and, in accordance with the historical cost convention, have charged against revenue in each of the last five years an amount of £20k in respect of depreciation. Since depreciation does not represent a cash outflow, they assured themselves that they were retaining within the firm a sufficiency of funds for the inevitable replacement of said assets when knackered. They now find that the RPI has doubled over the last five years and replacement will cost £200k. Simply to maintain Sweat Shops' asset base intact will require a capital injection of £100k into the company.'

(*Entrepreneurs start to snore.*)

'In addition, despite an effective credit control and debt collection system, Sweat Shops are encumbered with debtors. Again Sweat Shops lose out to inflation. Debtors always pay up in full but they are paying in money of a purchasing power lower than that which prevailed when the debt was incurred. But the accountant's tale is not exclusively gloomy. I was able to cheer Sweat Shops up by pointing out that they gain from their creditors and their bankers in that their long-term loan is at a rate of interest below the rate of inflation. In these cases, Sweat Shops are paying out pounds of a lower purchasing power than pertained when the debt was occurred. Alas, the proprietors of Sweat Shops failed to respond to these glad tidings and sent me on my way with a T-shirt inscribed "Historical Cost Accounting Stinks".'

(The accountant moves centre stage and raises his voice, not to wake the somnolent entrepreneurs, but, in truth, this is the biggest scene in his life and he is approaching his peroration. The entrepreneurs wake up, rubbing eyes.)

'In summary, you and many of your colleagues, not privy to the language of finance and its territory, have been fooled by (*pause for effect*) '*the money illusion.*'

'We have been fooled,' intone the entrepreneurs, 'by *the money illusion.*'

CURTAIN

* * *

Throughout the latter half of the 1970s the accountancy profession debated whether and how the historical cost accounts should be adjusted, or even abandoned, to take into account the effect of inflation on stocks, fixed assets, loans and monetary working capital (creditors and debtors). In the often acrimonious debate, three distinct viewpoints emerged, the fundamentalists, the ditchers and the hedgers.

The fundamentalists argued that the traditional concepts and conventions should not be altered in any way. Indices showed that, in the late 1970s, British industry was earning around 16 per cent on its trading assets. If the calculation were adjusted for the impact of inflation, the real return was a miserly 4 per cent. The effects of inflation were accepted but the answer lay not in destroying 'all things which are good and fitting' but in forcing managers to penetrate the money illusion and increase the rate of return to levels which did compensate for inflation. In other words, leave historical cost accounting alone and make larger profits. Politically, this approach was difficult. The most obvious route to increased profits lay through increased prices and, superficially at least, increased inflation at a time when governments were pre-occupied with the Retail Price Index. And, if profits did increase, in the confrontational culture of the UK, there would be pressure for higher wage awards.

At the opposite extreme, the ditchers argued that the impact of inflation was so elemental that an entirely new value-system needed to be constructed. The old system should be discontinued; traditional concepts and conventions were beyond adaptation and repair, and should be ditched.

The hedgers, in the mainstream of English culture, were for compromise. It was possible, they argued, to adapt traditional principles to meet the changed circumstances. The new could operate in tandem with the old and the linkages between the two could be made clear and demonstrable. This line of argument pleased neither fundamentalist nor ditcher but won the day. In truth, many accountants, like our entrepreneurs, were becoming exceedingly bored with the subject and the hedgers afforded a convenient end to tedium.

What emerged was the system of accounting known as CCA ('current cost accounting'). CCA was not to displace 'historical cost' (HC) accounts but was to operate in parallel with them. Annual financial statements for accounting periods which started on or after 1 January 1980 were to appear in both HC and CCA forms. At the centre of the CCA system was the concept of the operating capability of the business as reflected in its net operating assets (fixed assets, stocks, debtors and creditors). Any change in the input price of the goods and services which the firm used and was obliged to finance affected the amount of funds required to maintain the operating capability of these net operating assets. CCA modifies HC figures to reflect the impact of such price changes. It does so by making four adjustments to profit (before interest and tax) struck on an HC basis:

(a) Depreciation adjustment

This adjustment alleviates the problem of depreciation, based on historical cost, which does not reflect the increased price of asset replacement. Let us assume that a firm purchased an item of equipment for £40k in January 1983. In the course of the year, the government Statistical Services Index for that type of equipment increased by 10 per cent. The useful life of the machine is assessed at four years. Under HC conventions, the annual depreciation charge would be £10k. Under CCA, the current cost of the equipment is calculated by applying the relevant price index change to the HC of the item: £40k (×) 110/100 (=) £44k. On a straight-line basis, the current cost depreciation charge is £11k. The HC profit (before interest and tax) has had £10k charged as a cost for depreciation. Therefore, the current cost depreciation adjustment is an additional charge of £1k.

(b) Cost of sales adjustment

This adjustment, known as COSA, attempts to deal with the situation which laid the entrepreneurs of Piratical Products low. The adjustment is calculated by comparing the current cost of stock consumed in an accounting period with the historical cost of that stock. The adjustment reflects the excess of the former over the latter. Assume that a company buys a fixed volume of input materials every accounting period. The company maintains materials equivalent to two months' production in stock. In Accounting Period 11, Year 1, the cost of the materials purchases was £100k. Prices are rising at 1 per cent per month. Materials arëcharged to production on a first in, first out (FIFO) basis; the HC and the CCA treatment is as follows:

	Purchases (fixed volume)	Charged to production		
		HC	CCA	COSA
	£k	£k	£k	£k
Year 1				
AP 11	100			
AP 12	101			
Year 2				
AP 1	102	100	102	2
AP 2	103	101	103	2

The COSA, then, seals the gap which inflation creates between the cost of the input at the time of purchase and at the time of sale. If individual items of stock cannot easily be identified, and if the physical volume of stock is not constant, COSA is usually calculated by applying to the opening and closing HC stock figures the relevant price index for that category of stock. The 'averaging method' is commonly adopted. Assume the relevant index has risen from 100 to 110 in the financial year; an average is assumed at 105 and applied as follows:

	£	£
Closing stock	20,000 (×) 105/110 = 19,091	
Opening stock	16,000 (×) 105/100 = 16,800	
Price (+) volume change	4,000	
Volume change	2,291	2,291
COSA	1,709	

The averaging method reduces closing and opening stocks to a common price level. This indicates that, stripped of price level changes, volume has caused an increase of £2,291. The balance, £1,709, is the effect of price changes and represents the amount of COSA required to maintain operating capability intact.

(c) Monetary working capital adjustment (MWCA)

This adjustment measures the impact of price changes on debtors (unfavourable) and creditors (favourable). The treatment is similar to COSA. The averaging method is used and the relevant price index is usually the one applied to stock:

	Opening £	Closing £
Debtors	1,000	2,000
Creditors	500	1,000
Net monetary working capital	500	1,000

	£	£
Closing MWC	$1000 \times 105/110 = 955$	
Opening MWC	$500 \times 105/100 = 525$	
Price (+) volume increase	500	
Volume	430	430
MWCA	70	

The £500 increase in cash tied up in MCWA is a combination of volume changes and price-change effects. The averaging method quantifies the volume change. The balance must be the price effect and comprises the monetary working capital adjustment necessary to maintain intact the operating capability of the firm.

(d) Gearing adjustment

We have seen earlier the workings of 'gearing' or 'leverage' (Chapter 6). The gearing adjustment is more technical, less comprehensible than depreciation adjustment, COSA and MWCA. Once lenders become sensitive to high rates of inflation and anticipate that such rates will persist over time, interest rates rise to levels in excess of price changes to provide a 'real' return to the lender. If companies duly adjust HC profit for depreciation, stocks and monetary working capital to maintain operating capability, it can be argued that they are making two deductions in respect of that proportion of net operating assets which is debt-financed. The gearing adjustment removes this double-counting by crediting the CCA Profit and Loss Account with that proportion of the previous three adjustments which relates to debt-financed assets. The adjustment is calculated as follows:

	Opening £k	*Closing* £k
1. Long-term loan	50	50
2. Net operating assets	150	200
3. Gearing proportion:		

$$\frac{\text{average net borrowings}}{\text{average net operating assets}} = \frac{50}{175} = 28.6\%$$

4. The gearing adjustment is then calculated by multiplying the CCA operating adjustments (depreciation, COSA and MWCA) by the gearing proportion. The resultant figure is a credit in the CCA Profit and Loss Account.

The format of the CCA P & L Account, then, is as follows:

	£
Operating profit as shown in HC Accounts	x
LESS: current cost operating adjustments:	
Depreciation adjustment	x
Cost of sales adjustment	x
Monetary working capital adjustment (MWCA)	x
Current cost operating profit	x
ADD: Gearing adjustment	x
LESS: Interest	x
Current cost profit before tax	x
LESS: Tax	x
Current cost profit attributable to shareholders	x
LESS: Dividend	x
Retained current cost profit	x

So, has it all been worthwhile? Ralf Dahrendorf has detected in history a tendency to pose fundamental questions and then, before the issue can be fully resolved, to change the subject. In the case of inflation accounting, the tendency has been encouraged by a slackening of the rate of inflation in the 1980s. In true Parkinsonian fashion, the trend has been consistently downwards since the year in which CCA was introduced. The complexity of the system and its concepts has tended to limit its spread among non-accountants, many of whom were struggling to understand the machinations of historical cost accounting. The focus, in published accounts, is still very much on the historical cost figures with the CCA equivalents tucked away in technical obscurity at the back of the Annual Report. In these circumstances it is easy to become complacent and forget that rates of inflation of 7 per cent imply a doubling of prices every ten years.

It is not just the reduction in the rate of inflation which has encouraged history to change the subject. The rate of inflation has declined but the level of unemployment has risen and once again the UK is faced with a phenomenon, long-term mass unemployment, which was previously associated with other times and other places. Once again the territory of finance and its value-system is coming under fire. The 'balance sheet mentality' has been identified as a causal factor in the rise of unemployment. This mentality, it is argued, encourages firms to become leaner and fitter in pursuit of an increased rate of return on capital employed. The achievement of this objective is considered an end in itself and the 'externalities' are ignored. However, the route to an increased rate of return often lies through shedding employees and scrapping or mothballing plant and equipment. In conditions of high, long-term unemployment, the resources displaced, both human and inanimate, are unlikely to be used elsewhere to produce something of equivalent or greater value. Society loses the value of the production. Society, also, has to find the wherewithal for unemployment benefit and loses the revenue from taxation on earnings and profits. Quite apart from the social and human miseries of unemployment, if the 'balance sheet mentality' could be replaced by a system of accounting which recognized such externalities, it would be apparent that, in many cases, the protection of employment gave a better return to society than the condemnation of people to the dole queue. Society must throw off the fetters of the accountant's narrow view. Otherwise, large sections of British industry will be sacrificed on the high altar of finance. Here endeth the argument.

Now accountants, like most managers and specialists, do not feel comfortable with abstract issues like love, life and the meaning of the universe. Indeed, in modern managerial life, there is a category of questions to which the answers are so evident and predetermined that the question is best not put. Do you ever ask a barber if you need a haircut? A car salesman if the time is ripe to trade in your car? Mr Kinnock what he thinks of Mrs Thatcher? In similar vein there is little point in asking an accountant whether he thinks that the value-system should be recast to encompass wider social externalities. This state of affairs does not stem from any lack of sensitivity on the part of the accountant or from a perfectly natural reluctance to be branded a sociologist. Rather, the accountant subscribes to a value-system which prefers the concrete to the abstract, the practical to the theoretical. Under the money measurement concept, 'accounting records show only facts which can be expressed in monetary terms', the boundary is the 'business entity', and all else is 'immaterial'. Externalities are recognized insofar as they enter the revenues and expenses of the firm – redundancy payments, environmental expenses, rates and taxes. The accountant doubts whether the wider externalities could or, indeed, should be incorporated into this system.

If taunted further as 'the running dog of capitalism', 'the social scum, that rotting mass thrown off by the old society', or 'the bribed tool of reactionary intrigue', the accountant might open up and become philosophical. 'The purpose of a business,' he might say, 'is to do well rather than good. Indeed, by doing well, the business also does good; by doing well and serving customers' needs, it provides the funds for reinvestment which enable it to remain competitive and continue to provide employment to its people, markets for its suppliers and revenues to both local and central government. If the firm is required to put the 'good' before the 'well', the baby will have been dispatched as well as the bathwater. Let us first create the wealth before we argue about its distribution. Wider social issues are best left to the politicians. As a citizen, I will make due input to any political debate on these issues but essentially my job is to make the present system work, not get involved as an accountant in changing it.'

Making the existing system work better has been the objective of most initiatives in the field of 'social accounting'. The initiatives are based on a view of the business not as a naturally harmonious entity but as, potentially, an arena in which conflicting interests do battle. It may be argued that such a notion, at the macro-level, gave Karl Marx the idea for a book as long ago as 1848. But it was not until the 1970s that the 'stakeholder' concept gained wide currency in the UK. The concept identified a number of different constituencies which had a stake in the firm – investors, suppliers, customers, employees, community, government. Traditional financial statements were designed to meet the needs of the investor and to discharge management's role of stewardship over the shareholders' assets. These statements also provided useful information for customers and suppliers and for government in the determination of tax liability. But traditional financial statements seemed ill-adapted to the needs of the firm's potentially greatest asset, its workforce. The problem was not so much the amount of information to be disclosed as the form such disclosure should take. The end-product of the traditional statement, profit, was in English culture a word viewed with suspicion, associated with rewarding 'them' at the expense of 'us'. The notion of profit as the means of reinvestment in the firm was little understood. There lurked the suspicion that profit was simply trousered by directors and shareholders.

The concept of 'added value' was adapted to avoid the emotional connotations of the word 'profit' and to improve perceptions of the firm as an instrument of wealth creation. As we have seen, profit is measured as the difference between revenues and expenses, properly matched. Added value handles precisely the same data but in a different way. The added value approach distinguishes between expenses incurred within the firm and those incurred by purchasing the output of goods and services from suppliers outside the firm. The main components of internal expense are such items as wages, salaries, depreciation, interest, tax and dividend. External items comprise all bought-in goods and services. External expenses represent wealth created by people outside the firm. Hence the value added by the firm is represented by:

sales revenue (−) external expenses = added value

The difference of approach and its benefits are more easily illustrated by example. In 1983/4, our purveyors of bespoke schmutter, Sweat Shops, had sales revenue of £1,200k and expenses of £900k. These expenses were analyzed as:

	£k
Bought-in goods and services	300
Wages, salaries and employment costs	500
Depreciation	100
	900

In addition, interest payments of £50k were made and there was a tax liability of £100k. A dividend of £50k was payable.

The Profit and Loss Account would have taken the following form:

	£k
Sales revenue	1,200
Operating expenses	900
Operating profit	300
Interest paid	50
	250
Taxation	100
Available for distribution	150
Dividend	50
Retained profit	100

The added value interpretation of the same data is radically different:

	£k
Sales revenue	1,200
Bought-in goods and services	300
VALUE ADDED BY FIRM	900
Value distributed as follows:	
Employees	500
Investors (interest and dividend)	100
Government (taxation)	100
Reinvested to create further wealth (depreciation and retained earnings)	200

The added value approach, then, isolates the amount of wealth which has been created by the firm through the combined efforts of employees and investors. It also shows how this wealth has been distributed. And it does this without any recourse to the notion of profit. The concept of added value was much publicized and recommended in the late 1970s but reaction has been tepid. Where the approach has been applied, it has appeared very much as a subsidiary item in financial statements derived from traditional concepts and conventions.

Fundamental change is a long, slow and painful process in a traditional land like the territory of finance. The value-system develops mechanisms for survival. It is like a sequoia, constantly buffeted by gales: it learns to bend in such a way that it neither breaks nor becomes permanently deformed. In the territory of finance, fundamental change should not be rushed into, should not be embraced without due deliberation. Mao Tse Tung would have found it all eminently comprehensible. Asked for his opinion of the French Revolution, Mao pondered for a long time and finally replied, 'It's too soon to say.'

11. Punchlines

'If God were to give the company an enema, He'd stick the tube in Finance Department.'

Epitaph: Tomb of the Unknown Line Manager

We sit in the departure lounge and wait for our flights to be called. We have reached the end of our odyssey through the territory of finance. It is a time for nostalgia. We remember, with some embarrassment, initial problems with the language – assets and liabilities, revenues and expenses, cash inflows and outflows. We recall the odd vignette – dawn breaking over a balance sheet, a Profit and Loss Account wreathed in dark storm clouds. We reflect upon the occasional insight – why the balance sheet balances, the difference between cash and profit, the time-value theory of money. But, as we play the video of our journey in our heads, it slowly dawns on us that an essential element has been missing. We have been like an official mission to some authoritarian land. We have been shepherded around the factories and the farms, we have inspected the tools, the tractors and the technology, we have met the functionaries and the officials but the ordinary inhabitants of the land, the hewers of wood and drawers of water, have been no more than a vast and silent stage army. After all our peregrinations, we have little idea what makes the natives tick, what lights their candles and pops their corks. But to turn back now would be fatal: our seats are booked, the plane awaits, our hosts would be offended. We must attempt a more subtle approach. We shall glide mentally over the stage army and parachute silently down behind its lines. We shall infiltrate soundlessly from the rear and quietly observe.

In 1919, under the Paris Peace Treaty, the territories of Serbia,

Montenegro, Croatia, Dalmatia, Bosnia, Slovenia and Herze-govina were formed into the Kingdom of Yugoslavia. But 'balkan-ization' persisted and unity proved elusive. After the Second World War, under a different political régime, a fresh attempt was made to unite the nation. The chosen vehicle was a common language. A publicity campaign was duly mounted and the hoardings of the nation, from Split to Stip, from Ljubljana to Prilep, were emblazoned with a single slogan:

'Learn Serbo-Croat and let the Whole World understand you!'

The financial specialist views his specialism as the Serbo-Croat of the business world. Knowledge of his specialized language is the *sine qua non* of comprehending the workings of the business enterprise. Without such knowledge, vast areas of corporate life must remain devoid of meaning to the uninitiated. Now such a concentration of focus is not unusual among specialists. Most single-function specialists carry a torch for their own specialism:

SALES DIRECTOR: 'No one owes us a living. Cut-throat pressures. Icy blast of competition. We must sell or die!'

PRODUCTION DIRECTOR: 'But if we don't produce, we can't sell. Kick ass, move the metal, get the order out the door!'

PERSONNEL DIRECTOR: 'But the order will not progress through the door unless the people are happy. Motivation, human resource management, expansion and enrichment.'

RESEARCH DIRECTOR: 'All this is short-term. We must have vision. Where there is no vision the people perish.'

SALES DIRECTOR: 'But vision doesn't pay today's bills or fend off cut throat pressures and icy blasts of competition. We must sell or . . .'

We are trapped in a circular argument which will eventually disappear up its own premise.

To the accountant such discussions are interesting but not particularly useful. They are, in a sense, peripheral. For the accountant considers his specialism, finance, to have a higher order of meaning than any other specialism. Quite simply, finance is primordial. It provides the ultimate meaning for all the activities of the firm. It is universal in its import and supplies an underlying coherence to the apparently plural and discrete phenomena of the enterprise. Finance is both the motivating force and the common connecting element. It is the DNA of the body coporate.

Such a fundamentalist view of the enterprise can easily become the stuff of ideology. The principles invested in the view become the One True Way to which There is No Alternative. The problems of pluralism and diversity are avoided by being ignored. The ideology provides a comprehensive code within which all activities are allotted a predetermined position. There is one true system of reason, universally applicable. Allegiance to the system removes doubt and uncertainty: there is no need for indecision and compromise. The processes of decision-making are accelerated because, given the One True Way, discussion is redundant. Management is simply a matter of method and technique. The ideology determines the allocation of resources. The financial specialists are the zealots, 'the rest' the helots. So what's the problem?

The problem is two-fold:

(i) the facts don't necessarily fit the theory: finance is only one of the considerations which move the corporate muscle;

(ii) 'the rest', quite apart from a natural disinclination to embrace helotry, do not subscribe to the view that finance is the alpha and omega of the firm. They do not accept the ideology and are reluctant to accord primacy to the financial specialism.

How might an accommodation be achieved between the hammer of finance and the anvil of the other specialisms?

The arena in which such accommodation is sought is the political process of the firm. The financial specialist may doubt the need for politics and politicians but, as Adlai Stevenson pointed out, 'someone must fill the gaps between the platitudes and the bayonets'. In this arena are debated the crucial issues which cannot be resolved by the exercise of pure reason or by reference to the indisputable facts. By definition, these are multi-disciplinary issues. Through the political process we are seeking to encourage the accountant constantly to reinterpret his specialism in the face of the bayonets, slings and arrows of everyday managerial life. And we are seeking such accommodation with reality without destroying the accountant's dignity and without apparent departure from the Holy Writ of his fundamentalism. We are seeking to play Esau to his Jacob. 'The voice is Jacob's but the hands are the hands of Esau,' Genesis XXVII, 22. How might this be achieved? Let us observe the accountant at work.

Many specialisms develop an in-built sense of optimism for the future. If we learn from our mistakes in the past, we shall not repeat them in the future. Tomorrow will be better than today. The accountant does not necessarily demur. He simply requires proof and the pursuit of such proof can force 'the rest' into a corner. We have reached a hoary old set-piece of managerial life:

VISIONARY MANAGER (*pointing damning finger at accountant*): 'O ye of little faith
ACCOUNTANT (*unblinking*): 'Little faith but much experience.'

Sam Goldwyn once complained that he kept asking his accountant for information but all he ever got was figures. It is in quantified form that the accountant requires his proof. Visions, ideas and intuitions must first be turned into 'hard facts'. The 'facts' can then be converted into figures. Only then can judgements be made. Now the past is readily susceptible to such treatment but the future isn't. 'He who foretells the future lies even when he tells the truth.' But how can there be meaning without quantification? The accountant attempts to attribute meaning to future plans by trying, as far as possible, to relate these plans to *faits accomplis* in the past. This shows a proper respect for experience and enables the future to be viewed through a prism of what happened in the past under similar circumstances. A dash of the concrete is applied to the abstractions of the future. But the approach can seem restricting. To the visionary, the accountant appears to be burying the abstract under several tonnes of the concrete, to be seeking precision in situations where even approximation is difficult. The approach can also hint at risk aversion. Groucho Marx refused to join any club which would have him as a member. The accountant seems headed for a similar dilemma. He is only prepared to commit funds to those activities which will be self-financing. He has become the company's Abominable No-man.

The accountant, then, seeks to determine the 'hard', indisputable facts of any situation, however 'soft'. This predilection for the concrete provides the discipline whereby order can be fashioned out of chaos. Order is achieved through converting the 'hard' facts into 'hard' figures and shaping these 'hard' figures into the total system of the financial territory – balance sheet, Profit and Loss Account, cash flow statement. Planned activities are translated into assets and liabilities, revenues and expenses, cash inflows and outflows and everything is connected. This conceptual template is placed over the myriad planned activities of the firm and the future is revealed as an orderly set of inter-related figures. And the figures, in their serried ranks, take on a patina of reality. They seem to be so concrete. This *is* the future, neatly packaged and rigorously determined.

Time is also important. The future arranges itself into tidy blocks of time called financial years. Each financial year must be quantified well in advance. The generation of ideas should be synchronized with this timetable of quantification. For when the quantification has been completed, the emergence of subsequent ideas can only cause confusion. If the farmer has just planted wheat, subsequent arguments that he should have planted rape are redundant. And time is seen to pass in an orderly and measured manner. The future will be entered into by smooth progression. The image of the future is that of the spirit-level rather than the fiddler's elbow.

So what can upset this view of the future? In a word, events. Things happen but once things begin to happen the linkages between the figures in the financial system become apparent. A change in one item sets a chain reaction in motion. Accountants were well aware of the domino theory before the Vietnam War gave currency to the phrase.

As a result of the awful intrusions of reality, frustration can become the accountant's constant companion. First, the accountant detects, on the part of his non-financial colleagues, a conspiracy continually to change the corporate mind and render the determined indeterminate. The roots of this suspicion are antediluvian . . .

ACCOUNTANT: 'Mine is the oldest of the business specialisms. I take as my authority the Book of Genesis wherein God created order out of chaos. The prime function of the accountant is the fashioning of order out of chaos and you can't go back any further than Genesis. *Ergo*, mine is the oldest business specialism.'

OTHER SPECIALISTS: 'But who do you think caused the chaos?'

Secondly, the accountant experiences the frustration of those dedicated to making money not things. The accountant suspects that he is condemned to occupy the ante-room of history. Life must be lived at one remove from the action. As a result, the accountant feels responsible for reacting to events but powerless to determine their course.

Frustration can lead to repression, inner migration and the cultivation of a rich inner life. This may be good for the soul but not for the firm. The accountant may retreat into his profession and project himself as a professional who owes his allegiance not to the company but to his profession. Other managers in the firm are treated as clients, not colleagues. Or frustration can manifest itself in the games accountants play . . .

(a) 'Complex superiority':

This game, which contains four steps, has links with the basic tenet of Victorian child psychology: 'find out what he's doing and tell him to stop'. It is played as follows:

STEP 1. Compare a manager's actual performance with budget: if worse, criticize; if better, stay silent and move to Step 2.

STEP 2. Compare the manager's actual performance with last year: if worse, criticize; if better, stay silent and move to Step 3.

STEP 3. Compare the manager's actual performance with a

Japanese competitor: if worse, criticize; if better, stay silent and move to Step 4.

STEP 4. Deliver a homily on the dangers of complacency.

(b) 'Gulliverization':

The player is provided with a limitless supply of gossamer threads. Each thread is, in itself, insubstantial and easily broken. But if a large number of threads can be bound around the opponent before suspicions are aroused, the result can be total immobilization. So, a colleague puts forward an idea for a new line with estimated sales duly quantified. We shall use the gossamer threads labelled 'macro-economic factors'. In quantifying expected sales, on what basis has inflation been assessed? LBS, Henley, NEDO, Treasury Model, Gypsy Petulengo? Which version of money supply has been used? M3, M2, M1, M25? What exchange rate assumptions have been used? Dollar/sterling, sterling/basket of currencies, sterling/Matatutse gumbo bean? Having spun out the threads, consolidate with the gossamer strands labelled 'alternative scenarios'. So you've used the LBS forecast. What if you'd used Henley? You've focussed on the dollar but what about the mark? Etc., etc. Each alternative to be duly quantified. *Immobilisme*. Opponent trussed like a turkey, oven-ready.

(c) 'The double-headed penny':

This game has its origins in the Stalinist purges of the 1920s. Nikolai Karlovich von Meck, of the People's Commissariat of Railroads, set out to solve the post-revolutionary transport problem by increasing the average load of freight trains. He was shot as a 'wrecker'. His objective, obviously, was to wear out the permanent way and undermine the security of the Revolution. Shortly afterwards, his successor, Koganovich, actually implemented the policy and increased the average load. His opponents gleefully pointed out the implications for the permanent way. They were shot as 'limiters'. Their objective, transparently, was to throttle the potential of the Revolution. Praiseworthy performance can be a moving target. If you have not met budget, you can be criticized as a 'limiter'. But if you have exceeded budget, has it not been achieved at the expense of maintenance and morale which, in the longer term, will 'wreck' performance levels? Treat 'em mean and keep 'em keen.

Now none of these games makes particularly good spectator sport. Much energy and ingenuity is diverted in non-productive directions. The non-financial specialist is obliged to watch not only the competition but also his own back. Given that the behaviour stems from frustration, how can the accountant be led out of this state and re-integrated in the multi-disciplinary team?

The accountant sees himself as having constantly to react to the decisions and actions of others. Often he has little control or involvement in these actions and decisions. He is like Sisyphus pushing a financial rock up a hill. Just when he approaches the summit, when all the figures cohere in the financial system, something happens and the rock goes crashing into the valley below. Try to mitigate this feeling of reactivity. Cut him into the action at an early stage so that he can be warned of potential hazards and approach the summit by a different route. A cloud no bigger than a man's hand has appeared in the market. A foreign competitor is rumoured to be eyeing your patch. Warn the accountant. He can start doing the sums and providing for a sales shortfall throughout his system. The machine you planned to replace next year has developed a sickness which you fear may be terminal. Warn the accountant. Through the miracle of reallocation he may have unexpended capital allocations which can be diverted your way.

Above all, involve the accountant at an early stage in any new ideas. You have an idea for a new product or a new process. It is still a seedling in your mind, far from maturity. No matter. Go and talk. But first, prepare your pitch. Put on your accountant's head and try to see it through his eyes . . .

(a) Don't focus on the technical aspects of the project which interest you. Concentrate on the aspects that interest him. The 'worthwhileness' questions (Chapter 8) provide a framework:

   (i) what will it cost?

 (ii) how long will it take to implement?

 (iii) what annual revenues will it generate?

 (iv) for how long will these revenues continue?

 (v) what annual operating costs will it incur?

 (vi) are there alternative routes to the same objective?

 (vii) if so, what are the implications in terms of questions (i)–(v)?

(viii) what are the risks?

(b) Attempt quantification wherever possible but do not give the impression that you are upstaging the accountant's proper role in that process. Stress that you have done your homework. Appeal to his professionalism. Would he mind running his eye over the figures and making whatever adjustments he saw fit?

(c) Avoid 'softness'. Quantification will have provided some firmness. Try to relate the project to past developments, draw similarities with other projects. Give the accountant the opportunity to cross-reference your idea with something for which hard figures exist. Provide hooks which are embedded in accomplished fact rather than future abstraction.

(d) Do not give a 'bright lights and trumpets' presentation. Accountants prefer all inputs to be hard except sells. If you are considering the 'sunny side up' approach, remember that you are dealing with a profession imbued with the convention of conservatism. Accountants do not buy encyclopaedias on the door-step.

(e) Choose your time. Develop a sensitivity to the financial environment. Do not broach your idea just after the financial plans for the following year have been completed. If you do, the accountant will not be taking your words in. His mind will be concentrated on the sheer mayhem your idea will unleash on the financial system he has just topped out. Similarly, do not make your play when a previous project from your specialism has just dropped out of the sky. Allow a decent interval for the bereavement to be mourned. Attune yourself to the periods of receptiveness. There are times when the firm is in funds and is looking for outlets.

(f) Maintain the dialogue as you refine your idea. Use the accountant's expertise in refining the figures. Invite him into your specialism. Give him a share in the idea. When the final project submission is formulated, it will be a joint effort.

(g) Keep up the contact as the project goes live. Avoid surprises. If things start to go wrong let him know. He can start to make adjustments. Above all, do not conceal. Leave cosmetics to beauticians. If you do dissemble and are exposed, the accountant will play out his fantasy. When the fighting has died down he will enter the battlefield and proceed to bayonet the wounded.

Aboard the plane we fasten our safety belts. We are flying the national airline of the territory of finance – 'good food, good wine and a hint of fear'. We take off and circle the airport. One last look at the territory. We now know the people. Our knowledge is complete. We open the novel we have bought for the flight, P. G. Wodehouse. We begin to read . . .

> He was a chartered accountant and all chartered accountants have hearts as big as hotels. You think they're engrossed in auditing the half-yearly balance sheet of Miggs, Montague and Murgatroyd and all the time they're writing notes to blondes saying 'Tomorrow, one-thirty, same place.'
>
> *Ice in the Bedroom*, 1961

Appendix

Present Value Factors – Interest Rates

	1	2	3	4	5	6	7	8	9	10
					YEARS					
1%	.9901	.9803	.9706	.9610	.9515	.9420	.9327	.9235	.9143	.9053
2%	.9804	.9612	.9423	.9238	.9057	.8880	.8706	.8535	.8368	.8203
3%	.9709	.9426	.9151	.8885	.8626	.8375	.8131	.7894	.7664	.7441
4%	.9615	.9246	.8890	.8548	.8219	.7903	.7599	.7307	.7026	.6756
5%	.9524	.9070	.8638	.8227	.7835	.7462	.7107	.6768	.6446	.6139
6%	.9434	.8900	.8396	.7921	.7473	.7050	.6651	.6274	.5919	.5584
7%	.9436	.8734	.8163	.7629	.7130	.6663	.6227	.5820	.5439	.5083
8%	.9259	.8573	.7938	.7350	.6806	.6302	.5835	.5403	.5002	.4632
9%	.9174	.8417	.7722	.7084	.6499	.5963	.5470	.5019	.4604	.4224
10%	.9091	.8264	.7513	.6830	.6209	.5645	.5132	.4665	.4241	.3855
11%	.9009	.8116	.7312	.6587	.5935	.5346	.4817	.4339	.3909	.3522
12%	.8929	.7972	.7118	.6355	.5674	.5066	.4523	.4039	.3606	.3220
13%	.8850	.7831	.6931	.6133	.5428	.4803	.4251	.3762	.3329	.2946
14%	.8772	.7695	.6750	.5921	.5194	.4556	.3996	.3506	.3075	.2679
15%	.8696	.7561	.6575	.5718	.4972	.4323	.3759	.3269	.2843	.2472
16%	.8621	.7432	.6407	.5523	.4761	.4104	.3538	.3050	.2630	.2267
17%	.8547	.7305	.6244	.5337	.4561	.3898	.3332	.2848	.2434	.2080
18%	.8457	.7182	.6086	.5158	.4371	.3704	.3139	.2660	.2255	.1911
19%	.8403	.7062	.5934	.4987	.4190	.3521	.2959	.2487	.2090	.1756
20%	.8333	.6944	.5787	.4823	.4019	.3349	.2791	.2326	.1938	.1615
25%	.8000	.6400	.5120	.4096	.3277	.2621	.2097	.1678	.1342	.1074
30%	.7692	.5917	.4552	.3501	.2693	.2072	.1594	.1226	.0943	.0725
35%	.7407	.5487	.4064	.3011	.2230	.1652	.1224	.0906	.0671	.0497
40%	.7143	.5102	.3644	.2603	.1859	.1328	.0949	.0678	.0484	.0346
45%	.6897	.4756	.3280	.2262	.1560	.1076	.0742	.0512	.0353	.0243
50%	.6667	.4444	.2963	.1975	.1317	.0878	.0585	.0390	.0260	.0173

Acknowledgements

My colleague Bob Warner, Chief Accountant of the National Coal Board in South Wales, has given me much useful advice in the writing of this book. The following are the sources on which I have drawn most heavily for information:

General
Sizer, J. *An Insight into Management Accounting,* London, Penguin, 1969.
Reid, W. and Myddleton, D. R. *The Meaning of Company Accounts,* London, Gower, 1974.

Chapter 1
Morris, J. *Heaven's Command: An Imperial Progress*, London, Penguin. 1979.
Machiavelli, N. *The Prince*, London, Penguin.

Chapter 4
Brooks, J. *Business Adventures*, London, Penguin, 1971.

Chapter 5
Gage, W. L. *Value Analysis*, London, McGraw Hill, 1967.
Pyhrr, P. A. 'Zero-base budgetting', *Harvard Business Review*, Nov/Dec. 1970.
Pedler, M., Burgoyne, J. and Boydell, T. *A Manager's Guide to Self-Development*, London, McGraw Hill, 1978.

Chapter 6
Maas, P. *The Valachi Papers*, London, Panther, 1970
Galbraith, J. K. *The Great Crash*, London, Penguin, 1984.
Lever, H. and Edwards, G. Articles in *Sunday Times*, 1981

Chapter 8
Hall, P. *Great Planning Disasters*, London, Weidenfeld & Nicolson, 1980.
Mintzberg, H. 'Planning on the left side and managing on the right', *Harvard Business Review*, July/August, 1976.

Chapter 9
Mant, A. *The Rise and Fall of the British Manager*, London, Macmillan, 1977
Sampson, A. *Sovereign State: the secret history of ITT*, London, Hodder & Stoughton, 1973
Westwick, C. A. *How to Use Management Ratios*, London, Gower, 1981.
Mortimer, J. *Clinging to the Wreckage*, London, Penguin, 1983.

Chapter 10
Bagehot, W. *The English Constitution*, London, Fontana, 1965.
Bullock, A. *Hitler: a study in tyranny*, London, Pelican, 1962.

Chapter 11
Solzhenitsyn, A. *The Gulag Archipelago*, London, Collins, 1974.

Index

ATM is the only voluntary association of professionals in the UK whose work focuses exclusively on management training, education and organization development. Membership is open to anyone involved in this significant field of work. ATM's fast growth in recent years has created a lively membership of interested people in business, government, voluntary organizations, academic institutions and managerial consultancy.

The main aim of ATM is to promote high standards of management performance so that people in organizations and communities can work with greater effectiveness. Members are therefore encouraged to meet and collaborate to improve their own professional capabilities. Activities include evening and one-day meetings, and three- to four-day events held all over the UK and in Europe. These are designed to provide members with different developmental opportunities for the various stages of their careers. They also enable members to extend their knowledge and skills, to keep in touch with frontier thinking on management, and to exchange ideas and experience.

Free publications are sent to members. These include *MEAD* (*Management Education and Development*), a journal which has three issues a year and contains articles on current management training and development; frequent focus papers on topical issues; and a monthly newsletter.

For further information, contact:

ATM
Polytechnic of Central London
35 Marylebone Road
London
NW1 5LS

01-486 5811 (ex. 259)